THE McHENRY MANSION

MODESTO'S HERITAGE

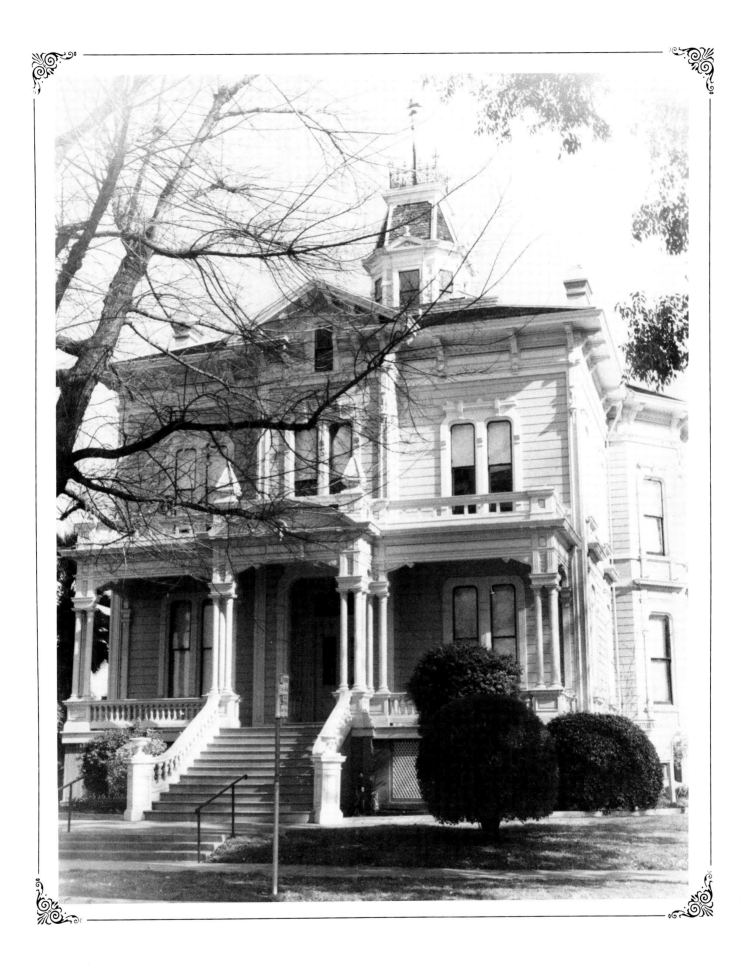

THE McHENRY MANSION
MODESTO'S HERITAGE
COLLEEN STANLEY BARE

McHenry Mansion Foundation Press
Modesto, California

Printed in the United States of America • First Edition

International Standard Book Numbers
Hard Bound Edition: ISBN 0-9615926-0-5
Soft Bound Edition: ISBN 0-9615926-1-3

CONTENTS

FOREWORD

This book began as a seemingly simple task, to present the story of one of Modesto's few remaining historical landmarks, a 100 + year old Victorian home. By its conclusion, it had evolved into a complex, many faceted research study of the building, its residents, and the environment in which it has existed. But what fun it has been, to relive life as it was in early Modesto and particularly in the house that Robert McHenry built.

I have attempted to achieve three goals in this project: to recreate the house in its proper setting, from the time of its construction to the present; to describe the lives of the individuals who lived within its walls; and to dispose of some of the myths about the house that have been repeated for many years. I have been careful to deal only with facts in the text and have not included stories or material that could not be authenticated. It will be noted that I have usually listed my sources of information and have refrained from making unsubstantiated generalizations.

The material for the book has been thoroughly researched and documented. It has been derived from many sources: interviews, city and county records, probate data, recordings of deeds and land acquisitions, census reports, cemetery records, the minutes of innumerable meetings of local boards of trustees and directors, personal letters, microfilm covering 50 years of newspaper articles located in a number of Northern California libraries, books and articles describing local history, city and county directories, and other archival materials. Specific documention will be found at the end of the book, in *Bibliography and Resources* and in the section titled *Chapter Notes*. The latter also contains additional information relevant to the text, for readers who are interested in greater detail.

All newspaper quotations are exact, including occasional misspellings, unfamiliar expressions, and noticeable lack of punctuation and capitalization. It is apparent that times have changed in the realms of journalism and grammar.

Through the years, the main subject of this book has been given a special title by the community: the *McHenry Mansion*. Even early day newspapers in the 1880s and 1890s referred to the structure as a "mansion". Therefore, in this text the house at 906 15th Street will be called the McHenry Mansion, or simply the Mansion spelled with a capital "M".

One of the earliest photos of the McHenry Mansion, circa 1885.

ACKNOWLEDGMENTS

This project could not have been realized without the assistance of many persons. Therefore, numerous "thank yous" are in order. The McHenry and Conneau families have been very supportive, and special thanks must be given to Merl McHenry whose recollections were very pertinent and valuable. Ora Louise McHenry Condrey and Arthur Ernest Conneau, Jr. also made important contributions. Wayne Mathes, Modesto City consultant for the restoration project, gave expert advice on that phase of the book. Those who read the text in its manuscript form made excellent suggestions, including three representatives of the McHenry Mansion Foundation: Frances Eakin, Shirley Elke, and Ronald "Bud" Stone; local historian Jeannette Maino; and several family members. The staff of the *Modesto Bee* rendered great assistance in publicizing my request for information about the sanitarium and apartment eras and the names of the apartment dwellers, and *Bee* Editor William L. McSwain and the *Bee* research librarians were particularly helpful. I am especially grateful to all of the wonderful phone callers who responded to the *Bee* articles and shared with me their memories of "life in the McHenry Mansion".

Many persons were interviewed (see pages 117) and I wish to say "thank you" to each of them, with particular mention given to: Ruth Hewitt Herbert of Farmington, who supplied important information about the Hewit family; Lois Huffman Jones of Merced who provided significant data about her grandfather, Charles Henry Huffman (see Chapter 2); and Derald and Dorothy Crabtree for their assistance with the apartment era.

The compilation of data for the book would not have been possible without the use of some of our fine Northern California libraries and museums. The reference librarians at our local Stanislaus County Library gave me invaluable assistance all through my research, and I constantly appreciated their spirit of helpfulness. Curator Heidi Warner and the docents at Modesto's McHenry Museum of Art and History were also very helpful, and I am grateful for the opportunity to copy valuable Museum photographs for use in the book. I appreciate the efforts of Lois Nish, who researched the McHenry family for a McHenry reunion held at the Museum in 1976. Berkeley's Bancroft Library and the Haggin Museum in Stockton both contributed to the project by allowing me to use their materials and by graciously giving permission for the reproduction of two photographs from their collections.

It is difficult to thank everyone who helped me in this endeavor, but I will attempt to name a few. In addition to persons already mentioned, and those interviewed (listings on page 117), these include: Harry Brown, Virginia Bruch, Tom Callaway and the Ticor Title Company, Pastor Robert H. Cowan (Seventh-day Adventist Church), Noreen Coyle and the Modesto City Clerk's office staff, Eloise Crary, Beverley Courtney (secretary, United Presbyterian Church), Dennis Dahlin (landscape architect, McHenry Mansion restoration), Herbert G. Florcken, Lou Gondolfo, Maree Hawkins and the Modesto Irrigation District staff, Dr. Catherine Julien (Curator, Merced Museum), Richard Ingle (Masonic Acacia Cemetery), Diane Keller, Loren Lacque (Masonic Lodge #206), Bill and Betty Nichols, Dr. Paul Pitman, Terrence Hansen (St. Helena Hospital Health Center), Dr. Donald La Tourette, Spiro Mellis, Peggy Mensinger, Margaret Painter, Carlyle Parker, Jean Pike, William Sigler, Stanislaus County Board of Supervisors records' personnel, and Rev. and Mrs. George Telle (United Presbyterian Church). Finally, the capable printers of this volume, Shirley and Richard Elke of Compass Maps, deserve special credit for their skill and patience in getting it all put together between two covers.

LIST OF ILLUSTRATIONS

PHOTOGRAPHS and Photo Credits

DRAWINGS

CHARTS

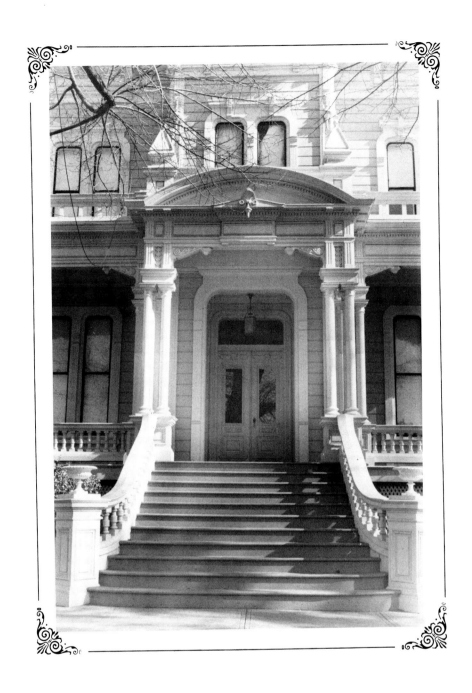

CHAPTER 1

A PLACE IN HISTORY

The northeasterly corner of 15th and I Streets in Modesto, California, was the scene of great activity in August of 1882. A large home was being built by one of the community's most prominent citizens, Robert McHenry. An item in the *Stanislaus County News,* dated August 25, described the project.

> The to be elegant and spacious residence of Mr. Robert McHenry on I Street is being rapidly erected, there being a large force of carpenters at work. The building, when completed, will be one of, if not the finest residences in the county, and will greatly beautify that poriton of Modesto in which it is located.

The construction of the home had been well orchestrated. The property had been purchased two years before, favorably located at the edge of the town on the widest street. Architectural drawings had been prepared, and the construction was to be supervised, by one of the San Joaquin Valley's leading architect-builders. The erection of the building that would later be known as the McHenry Mansion was well underway.

When Robert McHenry built his home in 1882-83, Modesto was not yet a town. It was still referred to as "Modesto Village". Established in 1870, with the coming of the railroad, the small settlement was not incorporated until August of 1884, about a year after Robert and Matilda McHenry moved into their new home. So the story of the McHenry Mansion reflects the history of Modesto, because the two evolved together. Today, this restored Victorian home is almost all that is left of Modesto's historical past. Most of the buildings of the period have been destroyed, and there is little remaining in this community to remind us of our heritage.

Standing tall on its mound of earth at 15th and I Streets, the McHenry Mansion has seen Modesto grow from a tiny village to a bustling city. How we wish that its walls could speak and tell us about life in the house and its surroundings as the town developed and grew out to it, around it, and eventually past it. But since houses can't talk, the story has had to be unearthed through research. And what a fascinating tale it has turned out to be!

The history of the McHenry Mansion can be divided into ten periods. Each reflects the changes that have occurred in Modesto since its beginnings over a hundred years ago. This is the story of a house -- and a town.

View of Front Porch

Robert McHenry.

CHAPTER 2

THE WORLD OF ROBERT McHENRY

On New Year's Day in early Modesto, it was the custom for some of the town's socially prominent ladies to entertain in their homes at what the *Stanislaus Weekly News* referred to as "calling" or "keeping open house". One of these was Mrs. Robert McHenry, who was reported to have opened her new home to callers on January 1, 1884 and to have "received calls from 1 to 9 p.m." on New Year's Day of January 1885. She again hosted an especially successful gathering on the first day of 1886. In the following *Stanislaus News* article dated January 8 of that year, note that husband Robert was present and participating although the party was entirely credited to his wife.

> At the elegant mansion of Mr. and Mrs. Robert McHenry, Mrs. McHenry received her friends cordially and entertained them in magnificent style. The large and richly furnished parlors were thrown open to callers and host and hostess exerted themselves to make all feel at home, and they succeeded too, for all went their way wishing Mr. and Mrs. McHenry many, many happy new years. The refreshments served at this place defy our descriptive powers. One could only appreciate them by being present and partaking of them.

Robert McHenry was a busy, successful rancher-business man who probably had little time for partying. By the time he constructed his house on the outskirts of Modesto in 1882-83, he had already led a full, productive life and was well on his way toward building the McHenry empire that would be carried on by his son, Oramil.

THE EARLY-MIDDLE YEARS, 1827-1883

Born on July 23, 1827 in Cambridge, Lamoile County, Vermont, probably of Scotch parentage, Robert McHenry moved to Ohio with his family in 1834 where he spent several years. Unfortunately, stories concerning the next phase of his life are conflicting, with several versions. The first comes from a group called the Stanislaus County Society of California Pioneers, of which he was a founding member and an officer in 1887. Following his death in 1890, the Pioneer Society adopted a memorial decree in his honor and issued a biographical description. It stated that, after 12 years in Ohio, Robert McHenry went to Mississippi in 1846 where he remained until January 1850. He then migrated to California and engaged in mining until 1852 when he settled in Stanislaus County. Another version of Robert's early years is from his obituary published in the *Stanislaus Weekly News*, stating that his move from Ohio was to Louisiana, after which he fought as a soldier in the fields during the Mexican War of 1846. He then came to California in 1849, did some mining, and soon settled in Stockton. A third version, in Tinkham's *History of Stanislaus County*, places Robert in New York before moving to Louisiana, with his migration to California via the Isthmus of Panama occurring ahead of the forty-niners. He then supposedly was involved in freighting in Stockton as well as mining at Chinese Camp. There is no way to know which of these histories is correct, but probably each contains elements of the truth. It definitely <u>is</u> known that Robert McHenry ultimately came to Stanislaus County and acquired 2,640 acres of land along the Stanislaus River that later came to be known as the Bald Eagle Ranch. In 1856, he was elected to a one year term on the Stanislaus County Board of Supervisors, which was only the second such board following its formation in 1854, and for a time served as its chairman. By then, the population of Stanislaus County was less than 1000, and the county seat was at La Grange. It would be another 14 years, in 1870, before the settlement of Modesto.

Meanwhile, Samuel Hewitt and his wife, Nancy, both born in Northern Ireland, had left their home in Steubenville, Ohio and, with their six children, traveled by wagon train across the plains to the area of present-day Farmington, California in 1853. One of the three Hewitt daughters, named Matilda Margaret but called "Tillie" by the Hewitt family, later married Robert McHenry. According to Ruth Hewitt Herbert, niece of Matilda Hewitt McHenry, the Samuel Hewitts followed the Immigrant Trail by Little John Creek near Farmington, arriving in the fall. They camped by the creek until the following spring, a trying experience because of unusually heavy rains. Samuel Hewitt homesteaded, planting his land to grain, and built a house. It was there, on a hot, windy autumn day in 1859, that an important event took place, as reported in the September 23 issue of *The Daily San Joaquin Republican* newspaper.

> ### MARRIED
> *At the residence of Samuel Hewitt, Esq., on Thursday morning, Sept. 22d, by the Rev. John A. Anderson, Mr. Robert McHenry, of Stanislaus County, to Miss Matilda M. Hewitt, of San Joaquin County.*

Robert and Matilda's son was called Oramil.

Home weddings were common at this time, in part because many churches had not yet been built. The Hewitts were Presbyterians, and the Farmington Presbyterian Church was not established until 1872 (later disbanded). On the day of their wedding the groom was age 32, and the bride was almost 21.

The newlyweds settled on the McHenry ranch and two years later, on November 14, 1861, their only child, Oramil, was born. In 1865, when his son was four years old, Robert McHenry helped to form the McHenry School District, the twelve grade school located at about what is today the junction of Patterson and Coffee Roads. The first class in 1865 had an enrollment of 35 pupils. This grew to 48 by 1869 when the teacher was paid a monthly salary of $70, including board, and Robert McHenry served as Clerk of the District. His address, as Clerk, was listed at Langworth, which was a flourishing little village located about 2½ miles west of today's Oakdale. The coming of the railroad to Oakdale in 1871 caused the demise of Langworth.

During this period Stanislaus County, without any irrigation, dry and hot in summer and averaging only 10 inches of rain a year, was considered ideal for wheat raising. The historical writers of the period (e.g. Bancroft, Branch, Elias, Smith, and Tinkham) described the San Joaquin Valley, including this county, as one vast, continuous wheat field. Wheat shortages in Europe, Argentina, and in the United States due to the Civil War, created a great demand for grain, and some local farmers with large acreages became wealthy. For several years, beginning in 1874, California exceeded all other states in the production of wheat, with Stanislaus providing a substantial portion. If Robert McHenry raised crops other than grain, no mention of it was made by the historians or in the newspapers. But by the mid-1870's, his name began to be associated with an entirely different endeavor, that of banking.

Robert McHenry's banking career probably began in about 1875 with his election as a director of the community's first bank, Farmers Savings Bank of Stanislaus County. This continued until the formation of the Modesto Bank in 1878, which merged with the Farmers Savings Bank, with Robert listed as one of the six directors of the new bank. In July of 1879, he became cashier of the Modesto Bank, which was the chief administrative officer. He also served as the bank's secretary-treasurer, and A.L. Cressey was president. One historian (Tinkham) suggests that Robert moved into Modesto at this time. This would certainly seem a possibility, because to make the six mile trip from the ranch to Modesto, perhaps daily, by horseback or carriage on poor roads ("dusty and full of chuckholes" to quote a news item) would have been taxing. Then in January of 1885, Robert McHenry became president and a director of the recently formed First National Bank of Modesto.

Several things happened in the late 1870s and early 80s to demonstrate the character of Robert McHenry. In September of 1878, he was one of several men who organized a meeting at the Courthouse in Modesto to help the victims of a yellow fever epidemic occurring in the Southern states. He was elected to an executive committee "to collect funds and transport them immediately to fellow citizens in the fever stricken district in this their dire distress". By the following January, the group had raised $1521.85, for a school fund to help the orphaned children of the victims.

Matilda McHenry was always known as a generous benefactor of the Presbyterian Church, but it was her husband, trustee Robert, who headed the committee to construct the church's first building in

BANK EELECTION - At the regular meeting of the stockholders of the Farmers' Savings Bank of Sanislaus County, held at this place last Saturday, the following Directors were elected: C. Dorsey, L.B. Walthall, S.P. Rogers, F.H. Ross, A.L. Cressey, Geo. W. Shell, J. Warner, R. McHenry, E.B. Beard, Wm. Enslen and Wm. Grollman. The proposition to increase the capital stock of the Bank was lost. C. Dorsey was elected President; L.B. Walthall, Cashier, and S.P. Rogers, Secretary.

STANISLAUS NEWS
January 8, 1876

The First Presbyterian Church, on the corner of 14th and I Streets, was dedicated in 1881.

Modesto, with Matilda and a Mrs. J.L. Armstrong serving as chief fund-raisers. Beginning in 1879, services were held in Modesto's local gathering place, Rogers Hall on H Street, until the white wooden church was built and dedicated at formal ceremonies on January 2, 1881. The site was on the corner of 14th and I Streets, just a block from the future McHenry home. The cost of the building, including furnishings, was $4,300, which was paid off in a few years, due in large part to the efforts of the McHenrys. Later that year, in October, Matilda helped to form, and was elected to the presidency of the church's first women's society, which they named "The E.F.s.".

By the 1870s Robert McHenry had become a leader in the cause for irrigation in the central valley, which would continue for the rest of his life. An article in the *Sacramento Record Union*, dated April 16, 1878, reported the filing of articles of incorporation for the Modesto Irrigation Canal Company, its purpose being "to convey water from the Tuolumne and Stanislaus Rivers in either of them over the lands comprised within the Modesto irrigation district". The principal place of business was to be in Modesto, and Robert McHenry was named as one of the company's seven directors. This was but one of a number of valiant efforts initiated to try to free the farmers from the constant threat of drought, resulting in disastrous crop loss, that occurred every few years. But all such schemes were destined to failure until the Wright Irrigation Act was passed in the state legislature in 1887. (see page 31)

In 1881, when his son Ora was age 20 and probably no longer in local schools, Robert McHenry became a trustee for the McHenry District School.

BUILDING THE HOUSE, 1882-1883

Modesto was only ten years old, and not yet incorporated, when Robert McHenry bought the initial property for his home from Charles Crocker of San Francisco on May 26, 1880. It is relevant to review the background of Modesto's beginnings in order to try to understand Robert's decision concerning that purchase.

The Central Pacific Railroad was extended to the site of present-day Modesto in October of 1870, and almost immediately a village was born. The land agent for the Railroad, originally called the Charles Crocker Construction Company and later the Contract and Finance Company, was given the responsibility of designing the town, as well as handling the purchase and sale of land. Its surveyors laid out the town parallel to the railroad tracks, in a pattern similar to that used previously for other villages. The one mile square town was divided into 300 by 400 foot blocks, each bisected by a 25-foot wide alley.

Every block was to contain 32 lots, 25 by 140 feet in size, and each street was to be 80 feet wide, except one. The exception was I Street with a width of 100 feet, because the Company intended that it become the town's main street. Streets running approximately north and south were designated by numbers, and those approximately east and west were named alphabetically. Lots in the little town were sold by the Contract and Finance Company until 1875, when those portions not yet disposed of were taken over by Crocker interests, which then handled all future property sales.

At the time Robert McHenry selected his homesite in 1880, a census report listed Modesto's population as 1693, and Modesto was referred to as a "village". The number of existing houses was small, and Robert had a great choice of possible locations. Therefore, it is significant that he chose to place his home on the corner of 15th and I Streets, I being the widest street in town. The site was on the outskirts of the village, which only extended about four blocks in any direction from the main business center on H Street between 9th and 10th. It was also about six blocks from the notorious "dens of vice" in the area adjacent to the railroad tracks called "The Front", where 9th Street is today. And, it was just a block from the Presbyterian Church, which he and his wife had been instrumental in building. He purchased five lots, #17 through #21 in Block #122, for $425, which would have represented an area 125 feet wide by 140 feet deep. This must not have seemed quite adequte for the 54 by 80 foot structure because, as construction got underway, Robert McHenry bought another lot, #22, for $75 from Charles Crocker in August 1882. The following year, in August 1883, a Richard Barnes acquired, from Crocker, the neighboring lots #23, #24, #25, and #26 in Block #122 for $300. Finally, on February 14, 1887, four years after the completion of his home, Robert McHenry bought lots #23 through #26 from Richard Barnes for $700. Barnes therefore made a 133⅓ per cent profit on the sale, and Robert then owned a total of ten lots, comprising 250 feet of property or about one third of the block, at 15th and I Streets.

We can only speculate as to how Robert McHenry made the choice of the architect-builder for his house. Again, an historical event probably played a role in his decision. In a spirited election held on September 6, 1871, the citizens of Stanislaus County voted to have the county seat moved from Knights Ferry to Modesto. Other county seats had been at Adamsville (now defunct), Empire, and La Grange. County records were quickly transported in three wagon loads from Knights Ferry to Modesto, to be housed in temporary quarters, and there was an immediate migration of county officers and lawyers. Now a permanent courthouse was urgently needed in the busy little village. In 1872-73, a handsome three story building, designed by San Francisco architect A.A. Bennett, was built by Robinson Brothers contractors of Stockton, on the 11th and I Street block that had been donated to the town by the Contract and Finance Company in 1871. Described by writer L.C. Branch as "a beautiful building" and by the *Stanislaus*

County News as "one of the best pieces of public work in the state for the money expended", the courthouse clearly was considered a success. The contractors, Robinson Brothers, received special praise from author Tinkham who wrote that "both men were mechanics such as today one will seldom find". In 1874, practically identical courthouses were built in Merced, Fresno, and Bakersfield using the Bennett design.

In 1879 one of the Robinson brothers, named Jeremiah or Jerry, began to advertise in the local newspapers. It is noteworthy that, in the December 19, 1879 issue of the *Stanislaus County News,* an advertisement for "Jerry Robinson, Builder and Contractor", appeared directly under the Modesto Bank advertisement which listed Robert McHenry as cashier. If Robert were contemplating building a house (which would seem likely, since he bought his property just six months later), he might well have noticed the announcement beneath his name that read, "Plans drawn and estimates made. Work in country solicited and personal attention given". By November 1881, the Robinson advertisement had changed. "Jerry Robinson, Architect and Practical Builder, plans drawn, estimates made, and buildings erected on reasonable terms". During this same period, Jeremiah Robinson also did similar advertising in the *Stockton Daily Independent* and the *Stockton Mail* newspapers and in the San Joaquin County and Stockton City Directories. In the directories of 1881 and 1883-84 he spelled his name "Jere", but in subsequent directories, as late as 1906, he was listed as "Jeremiah" and "Jerry". The other Robinson brother, Mayhew, was referred to as "carpenter with Jere Robinson" in the 1881 directory, although both men had been carpenters in Stockton for many years, dating back to at least 1856.

Jeremiah Robinson was the architect-builder. (Collection of Haggin Museum, Stockton, CA).

Several facts are known about this man, Jeremiah Robinson, who designed and built the McHenry Mansion. Like Robert McHenry, he was a member of the Society of California Pioneers, except that his affiliation was with the San Joaquin chapter which was formed in 1867. Records of the Society's minutes indicate that Jeremiah Robinson was originally from Massachusetts and arrived in California on October 9, 1849, having traveled via Cape Horn on the ship Walter Scott. During the time that he was building the McHenry house (1882-83), he was on the Board of Directors of the San Joaquin County Pioneer Society and the following year (1884-85) served as the group's president. In the 1890s he again was a director and second vice president (1898-99).

Jeremiah Robinson advertised in the City and County Directory of San Joaquin, Stanislaus, Merced, and Tuolumne, 1881.

A news item of June 2, 1882 marked the beginning of the McHenry construction. "Mr. Robert McHenry is preparing his lots on I Street near the Presbyterian Church, preparatory to the erection of one of the finest residencees in the county". Another *Stanislaus News* article, dated August 4, is even more interesting.

> A large force of workmen are engaged in the erection of Mr. McHenry's new residence. The building is to front I Street and is a short distance from the Presbyterian Church. Jerry Robinson of Stockton is the architect and superintendent of the work. It is to be constructed by day labor, instead of the contract plan and, undoubtedly, when finished will prove to be the finest and most costly residence in Stanislaus County.

The October 1881 issue of the *California Architect and Building News* recommended that architects set their fees at 5 per cent of the total building cost for "full professional services including supervision", although other issues of the journal lamented the fact that architects often settled for less. The plans probably included the building of a barn and stables on the property, as well as a windmill and a tank house.

This story would not be complete without a consideration of how the lumber, consisting of redwood siding for the exterior and fir for the rest of the house, must have been acquired. The May 1882 *California Architect and Building News* noted that redwood was a very popular building material at this time, in part because the redwood trees were so much larger than other timber in Western forests. Logs at the mills at Humboldt Bay averaged over seven feet in diameter and, the journal stated, "we have frequently seen trees cut into logs that would make in lumber at the mill over 100,000 feet". Redwood was also inexpensive and easily obtained from the native trees on the upper California coast, according to Clarkson B. Bradford, Jr., president of the Modesto Lumber Company which was originally established in 1878 at 9th and G Streets. During an interview, he stated that, in the 1880s, redwood bound for Modesto was brought down the coast to Stockton on ships called lumber schooners. From there, the lumber was carried by steamer, or on boats referred to as "scows", down the Tuolumne River to locations along the banks near the old 9th Street railroad bridge. Then it was loaded onto horse-drawn wagons and

An early view of the Mansion taken on a gray winter day.

transported to the building sites or the lumber company. The fir used in the Mansion's foundation, floor joists, and framing of the house, would have been brought to Modesto by rail, from Washington State or possibly from Oregon.

The basement of the McHenry Mansion has been the subject of considerable interest because of its early use as servants' quarters and later for laundry and heating equipment and as an apartment. Its digging would have been the first step in the actual construction of the house, and it is of value to consider how such a large area could have been dug without the benefit of heavy equipment. The most common method during the early 1880s was by hand, with a crew of men using picks and shovels. However, it is possible that the basement could have been scooped out using some type of dirt scraper attached to a team of horses. One such tool, called the "Fresno Scraper", was invented by James Porteous in Fresno about this time. The foundation and outer walls of the basement were built with red brick, as well as the interior walls that served as dividers for seven finished rooms. The brick was then covered with a thin coating of light colored plaster. The rooms were separated by brick archways that anchored the framework for doorways, and each of the load bearing brick walls was constructed so as to support walls directly above on the first and second floors. Beaded tongue and groove fir boards covered the ceiling, and the flooring was of tongue and groove painted wood. It is interesting that, in size and shape, the basement is a duplicate of the floors above it.

Some of the non-lumber materials for the McHenry house may well have been purchased at various stores in town. Wood & Turner advertised "shelf and wooden hardware" and also sold nails, undoubtedly the square type that were used in the McHenry Mansion. Howell & Maze specialized in plumbing, a "full line of kitchen utensils and tinware", and were "solo agents" for the Superior Range described as "the best in the market". Jamison & Reedy sold gas fixtures, as well as stoves (such as the Hub Range) and tinware. William Fraser did well-boring, claiming "wells bored to any depth or size at 25 cents a foot", and the Machine Shop located on G street, between 10th and 11th, sold windmills and pumps.

An important aspect of the building of the McHenry Mansion would have been its decorating, painting, and final finishing. Although Modesto supposedly had four paint stores during this period, including Wood and Turner that touted "paints, oils and varnishes", it is entirely possible that Stockton architect Jerry Robinson might have led Robert McHenry to that city for assistance in the detailing of his house. Stockton was settled in 1847, 23 years before Modesto, and already had a population of 2000 by 1850 and 14,000 in 1890. Modesto's early day newspapers frequently described train trips made by local citizens to Stockton, occasionally mentioning the McHenrys, where there were many more stores and greater shopping facilities. For example, nothing printed in the Modesto newspapers compared with the advertising done by Badger Brothers, wallpaper hangers, in the *Stockton Daily Evening Herald* and *The Stockton Mail* during 1882 and 1883. Located at 200 Main Street, the firm advertised "plain and decorative paper hangers, the finest and largest stock of papers in Stockton, plain and ornamental painting and artistic frescoing, all work strictly first class" and modestly claimed "the finest frescoing to be found in the State". The Modesto Lumber Company ordered materials from a number of Stockton firms during this period. One of these was P.A. Buel & Company on Center Street, dealers and manufacturers of mouldings, balusters, newell posts, rails, moulded doors, bay windows, window frames, pickets for fences, and other such items.

The McHenry house had gas lighting and indoor plumbing from the beginning. Although a water company and a gas works were erected in Modesto in 1876, both accommodated users only in the immediate downtown area. The home probably had its own gas plant, and there is evidence that gas lines and jets were installed in most of the rooms at the time of construction. It also had a water system, most likely consisting of a well, windmill, and one or more water storage tanks located either in a tank house or in the attic. Hot water for the bathrooms was provided by free standing, nickel plated gas heaters, a luxury not without risk since this type of heater sometimes blew up. There were at least two brick-lined cesspools for sewage disposal on the property, which were discovered during the restoration, cesspools being the town's only method of dealing with this problem in the 1880s. It is known that coal-burning fireplaces and coal or wood-burning stoves provided heat for the house, with a large wood stove utilized for cooking.

The beautiful clean lines of the Mansion.

The house was designed in the Victorian Italianate style, sometimes referred to as the "bracketed style" because of the elaborate brackets placed under the eaves. It encompassed 10,080 square feet of interior space, and reports indicate that the home was Modesto's largest and finest when it was built. The first floor, with its 13 foot 3 inch ceilings, consisted of a front parlor, back parlor, library, dining room, kitchen, office, bathroom, two entry halls, an interior hall, and three porches. The second floor, with 12 foot 3 inch ceilings throughout, included a sitting room, six bedrooms, and a bathroom, with a central hallway. A sleeping porch was added later. Two staircases, located in the front and rear of the building, led to the second floor, with only the back staircase continuing up to the third floor attic. The basement was entered by a separate stairway off of the back hallway and by another outside entrance at the rear of the building. The first floor of the house was constructed about 5½ feet above the level of the ground, making it possible to have 2½ by 3 foot windows in the basement's exterior walls. These afforded full daylight to the finished rooms. The attic, which was used for storage, also covered the entire area of the house and was topped with the eight-windowed octagonal cupola that has become the symbol of Modesto's McHenry Mansion. There was a floor in the cupola, reached by a stairway in the center. Landscaping included an orange grove on the east side of the house, citrus trees being common in Modesto Village, with Elm trees planted along both 15th and I Streets. Photographs taken in the mid-1880s show that the house was encircled by a three to four foot wooden fence.

THE ORIGINAL HOUSE

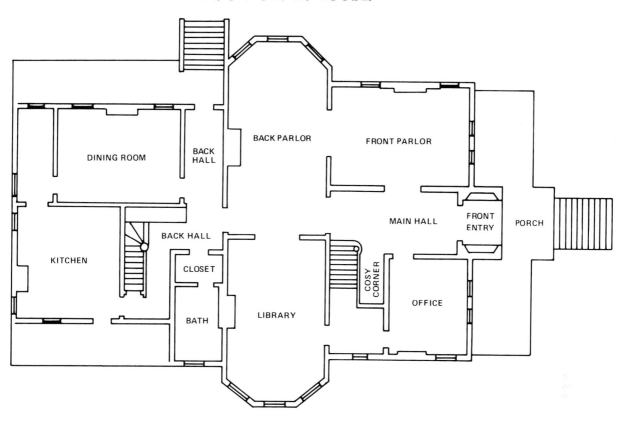

FIRST FLOOR

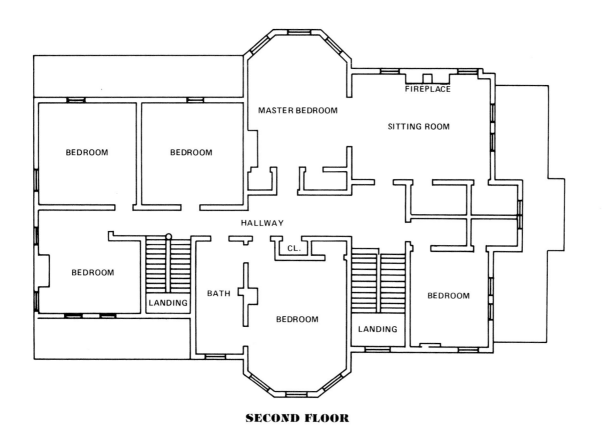

SECOND FLOOR

THE STORY OF THE TWIN HOUSE

STANISLAUS COUNTY NEWS
June 26, 1890

A frequently repeated, undocumented story about Robert McHenry's building of his house is worth noting. It claims that he had a friend who built a house for $11,000 and that Robert bet the friend that he could build his own house for $10,000. Robert supposedly succeeded and won the wager. The obvious care with which Robert McHenry planned his house, the purchase of the lots two years in advance of construction and the hiring of an architect-builder, plus his apparent conservative nature, would seem to negate the idea of his having made such a frivolous bet. However, if some sort of wager ever did occur, it might have been with Charles Henry Huffman of Merced, who built a home in that city at about the same time. C.H. Huffman was Robert McHenry's brother-in-law, having married Matilda Hewitt McHenry's sister, Sarah Ann Hewitt. Their wedding occurred at the Samuel Hewitt residence near Farmington on October 30, 1855, just four years before Matilda married Robert in the same setting. Sarah later died in childbirth, leaving Huffman with three children. He was occasionally mentioned in the *Stanislaus County News* as a visitor to Modesto, as was Robert McHenry a visitor to Merced, and was among those present at Robert's and Matilda's funerals. The youngest of C.H. and Sarah Huffman's children, Milton, was also listed as a witness and "second groomsman" at the marriage of Oramil McHenry to Louise Bilicke in 1886.

Charles Henry Huffman was a very successful wheat rancher and, with Charles Crocker, developed the water system that later became the Merced Irrigation District. He also was the founder and first president of the First National Bank of Merced in 1887. He built his house on the huge Huffman ranch near Merced's Bear Creek. The fascinating aspect of this story is that, at least on the exterior, the Huffman house was almost identical to the McHenry house. An article in the *Merced Sun* newspaper of January 12, 1933, describing its destruction by fire, reported that construction on the house began in 1882 with completion in 1883, the same dates as for the McHenry Mansion. Lois Huffman Jones, a Merced native and Huffman's granddaughter, stated during an interview that the builder of the house was a young German immigrant named Lewis Wegner, who later constructed many homes in Merced and went on to become the town's mayor. It is thought provoking to consider the possible meaning of the apparent simultaneous construction of almost twin houses by these two enterprising banker-ranchers who were related by marriage. Could they have used the same architectural plans for the design of their homes? Of course, we will never know. But an interview with Elmer Murchie of Merced, a retired Crocker-Huffman Water and Land Company superintendent, revealed some details about the house. Murchie started working for the Company in 1909, and one of his first tasks was to measure the Huffman home for the installation of electricity. He stated that the basement contained several completely finished rooms, each with fireplaces, occupied by the servants. It also included the kitchen, and food was

Photo of the Huffman house. (Courtesy, Bancroft Library)

Twin photo of McHenry house.

taken up to the first floor by means of a dumb waiter. The main floor, where the family lived, had large parlors and the dining room. The bedrooms were on the next floor, and above this was a ballroom wrapped around the base of the cupola tower which extended down into the building. The house probably had about 30 rooms, and there supposedly were fireplaces in each room as well as in the finished livery stable. At a later date the property included tennis courts, a swimming pool, a green house, vegetable and flower gardens, and other outer buildings. Charles Henry Huffman left Merced for San Francisco in 1893, and his house became the headquarters for the Crocker-

Huffman Company. Referred to as "The White House" in the community, the home was occupied by a number of Company superintendents and their families for many years before it burned to the ground in 1933.

LIFE IN THE McHENRY HOUSE

It is interesting to speculate on life as it existed within the walls of the new McHenry home in the 1880s. It is known that during a later period, the family used the I Street entrance to the house rather than the more formal 15th Street door. This custom may well have been started by Robert and Matilda. The double parlors on the first floor were typical of the finer homes in Modesto at this time, with the front parlor reserved for "company" and closed off by sliding doors when not in use. Both parlors would have been utilized for parties and when there were guests, with the library also in use for larger gatherings such as during the New Year's Day open houses. Family meals were served in the dining room, adjoining the kitchen and pantry area. Upstairs, on the second floor, the front southeast room was presumably a sitting room, just as it was in the early 1900s. This was one of the most pleasant rooms in the house because of its southern exposure and excellent view of the town. During the cold winter months it would have been filled with sunshine, with the fireplace furnishing additional warmth. There were stoves in each of the other rooms upstairs, in which either wood or coal was burned for heat, with the flues attached to the home's chimneys. The master bedroom was probably next to the sitting room, although it is known that the bedroom across the hall, adjoining the bathroom, fulfilled that role at a later time. The bathroom also had a second door opening into the hall. The other bedrooms would have been used by guests and son Oramil, who was 22 years old by the time the McHenrys moved into their new home. Coal was burned in the home's six fireplaces which was delivered free by the City Coal Yard, priced at $5.50 a ton for Ione coal, $14 a ton for Seattle coal, and $16 for Sidney (Australia) coal. In Modesto's early days, a large Chinese settlement was on the west side of town in the area of 7th and 8th and F and G Streets. Here much of the town's laundry was done. Families like the McHenrys had their laundry picked up and later returned every week by Chinese launderers, a practice that continued for several decades.

Few facts exist concerning how the house was furnished, except that its furnishings were referred to as "elegant", "rich", and "beautiful" in the newspapers. One local furniture store during this period, called Deyoe and Devendorf's, advertised "lounges and upholstered chairs, carpeting, oil cloths, and mattice" and could have served the McHenrys. It also proclaimed, "We propose to sell our goods at prices that will compare with San Francisco, saving our patrons the expense of railroad fare and freight". It is known that some affluent Modestans had their homes furnished and decorated by San Francisco firms such

This stove flue was attached to the chimney in an upstairs bedroom.

26

as W. & J. Sloane & Company. Located at 641 to 647 Market Street, Sloanes advertised oriental, American, and English rugs, carpets, furniture, and upholstery. A third possibility exists, which again has to do with Stockton. For example, a store which had its own factory, as well as handling furniture from the East, was Sylvester, Moye & Company, with showrooms at 250 and 252 Main Street and a factory at California Street between Main and Market Streets in Stockton. In the 1882-83 *Stockton Daily Evening Herald* newspaper advertisements, the firm described itself as "headquarters for furniture, carpets, and upholstery goods, with a large line of new patterns in solid walnut, ash, maple and pine bedroom sets, desks, sideboards, secretaries, hall stands, etc.". It also featured parlor sets, lounges, and easy chairs, and "a full line of Brussels, tapestry, and ingrane carpets always on hand and new patterns constantly arriving".

It is not known how many servants were hired by the McHenrys, but during a later period there was a cook, at least one maid, a groom to care for the horses and drive the carriage, and one or more persons to tend the grounds. Although Matilda McHenry probably selected the days' menus, undoubtedly it was the cook who traveled in a horse-drawn buggy on the dirt streets to purchase food at a store like "A. Minottis, Grocery and Provisions" on 10th Street. Many of the items at Minottis were sold in bulk where one dollar would buy 12 pounds of sugar, 14 pounds of brown syrup, 10 cans of tomatoes, 12 pounds of Carolina rice, or 5 cans of table fruit. Other prices included bacon, 14 cents a pound; eggs, 15 cents a dozen; Oregon potatoes, 1 cent a pound; pickles, $1.25 a keg; and tobacco, 50 cents per plug.

The conversation around the McHenry dinner table during the last half of 1883 may well have included concern for the welfare of United States President James Garfield, who was shot on July 2 and died 80 days later. He was replaced by Chester Alan Arthur, and Grover Cleveland was elected to the office in 1884.

THE LATER YEARS, 1884-1900

It is important to understand the conditions in Modesto Village during this period, in order to place Robert McHenry's very productive last years in proper context. By all accounts, life in Modesto in the 1880s was, at best, a challenge.

At about the time the McHenrys set up housekeeping in their new home, Modesto was in what historian Sol Elias called "a deplorable state". There were no sidewalks, except for wooden planks that several merchants had put down in front of their stores in the business district. One January news item complained that the sidewalks and crossings were almost "impassable" due to water and mud. The ungraded, rutted, littered streets were muddy in the winter and dusty in the summer. Street cleaning and garbage collecting were entirely left to private enterprise, and pigs, horses, and cattle roamed through the town at will. There were no lights, so people carried lanterns at night to find their way and to protect themselves against thieves.

Moreover, at the beginning of this period, the village had no municipal government and was lawless and disorderly, controlled by the Front Street saloon crowd. Wealth garnered from the huge wheat crops poured into the little town and was spent by the harvesting crews at the saloons and gambling halls. Sol Elias wrote,

> The Front was wide open both day and night. It was the rendevous of the most daring sports, gamblers, and saloon hangers-on that could be gathered together in the state. Gambling and drunkeness were rampant. Hardly a night passed but some farmhand was fleeced in a game of cards, robbed and beaten up, plied with liquor or doped, until he became insensible and his pockets picked by the light-fingered gentry. Carousals made the night hideous. So many were the murders the town had the reputation throughout the state of being a place in which there was literally a man served for breakfast every morning.

About this time, a group calling itself the Vigilantes, and later the San Joaquin Regulators, took the law into its own hands and, on several occasions, raided the gambling halls, opium dens, houses of prostitution, and dance halls. The most dramatic raid occurred in March 1884, during which a notorious saloon keeper named Joe Doane was killed. This was also the year of a disastrous fire, destroying many downtown buildings, which inadequate fire equipment with a rotted water hose could not control, another event that demonstrated the need for organized local government.

It was in this somewhat turbulent setting that Robert McHenry and other industrious, law-abiding people were leading quiet lives while working to improve their little town and make it more livable. In July of 1884, Robert participated in a lively meeting at Rogers Hall, called for the purpose of nominating a slate of governing officers. On August 1, an election was held, resulting in the formation of Modesto's first government and the incorporation of the town.

Meanwhile, during these years following the building of his house, Robert McHenry led a vigorous life. In January of 1884, he was reelected to the position of cashier at the Modesto Bank, with J.R. Broughton serving as assistant cashier. The First National Bank of Modesto was founded in June 1884, and in January 1885 Robert became its president. At this time he was replaced as cashier of the Modesto Bank by Broughton, although he remained as a director on the boards of both banks until just before his death in 1890. Serving with him as officers of the First National Bank were W.B. Wood, vice president, and S.P. Rogers as cashier. Later, in about 1890, the Union Savings Bank was organized as an adjunct to the First National Bank, with the same officers serving both banks.

In the mid-1880s Robert made a number of trips to San Francisco, described in the *Stanislaus News* as a four-hour train trip, and also went to Merced and made one excursion to Texas. Santa Cruz became a popular summer destination for Modestans, as an escape from the valley heat, and the McHenrys joined the exodus to that city as well as to Monterey. In August 1885, the McHenry family left for the coast, with Robert returning a week later and Matilda in five weeks. A com-

At the annual meeting of the stockholders of the Modesto Bank, held at this place last Saturday, the following officers were elected: Directors, A.L. Cressey, Robert McHenry, Isaac Perkins, Wm. Enalin, E.B. Beard, J.F. Kerr and J.R. Broughton; President, A.L. Cressey; Cashier, Robert McHenry; Assistant Cashier, J.R. Broughton, vice S.P. Rogers; Bookkeeper, Frank A. Cressey, vice Broughton, promoted.

STANISLAUS COUNTY NEWS
January 18, 1884

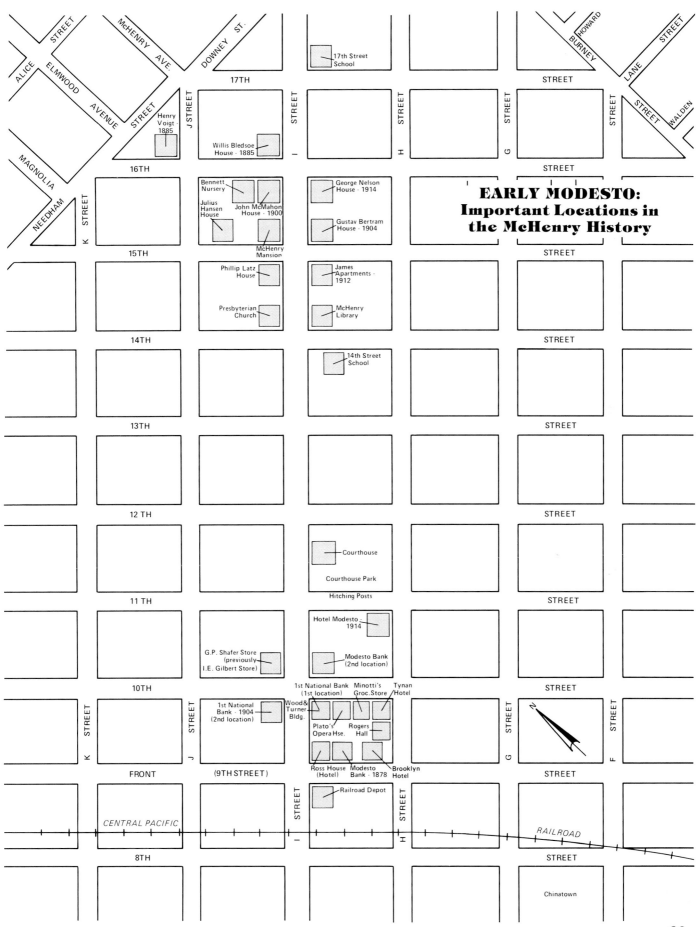

EARLY MODESTO:
Important Locations in
the McHenry History

ALICE STREET

ELMWOOD AVENUE

STREET

McHENRY AVE.

DOWNEY ST.

MAGNOLIA

NEEDHAM

BURNEY

HOWARD STREET

LANE STREET

WALDEN

J STREET

17TH

17th Street School

STREET

STREET

H STREET

STREET

G STREET

STREET

STREET

Henry Voigt 1885

16TH

Willis Bledsoe House - 1885

K STREET

Bennett Nursery

Julius Hansen House

John McMahon House - 1900

McHenry Mansion

George Nelson House - 1914

Gustav Bertram House - 1904

15TH

Phillip Latz House

Presbyterian Church

James Apartments - 1912

McHenry Library

STREET

14TH

14th Street School

STREET

13TH

STREET

12 TH

STREET

Courthouse

Courthouse Park

Hitching Posts

11 TH

STREET

G.P. Shafer Store (previously I.E. Gilbert Store)

Hotel Modesto - 1914

Modesto Bank (2nd location)

10TH

K STREET

J STREET

1st National Bank - 1904 (2nd location)

1st National Bank (1st location)

Wood & Turner Bldg.

Plato's Opera Hse.

Minotti's Groc.Store

Rogers Hall

Tynan Hotel

STREET

G STREET

F STREET

N

FRONT

(9TH STREET)

Ross House (Hotel)

Modesto Bank - 1878

Brooklyn Hotel

STREET

STREET

I STREET

Railroad Depot

H STREET

CENTRAL PACIFIC

RAILROAD

8TH

STREET

Chinatown

29

mon method of travel to Santa Cruz was by train, via San Jose. 1885 was also the year when Ora was thrown from his buggy, as his horse became frightened and ran away. Only the buggy was injured, on the top and back.

The little town continued to prosper and a news item noted, "Modesto begins to wear the appearance of a thrifty young business city. She has more fine business blocks than any town of her size in the state". One fall day in September 1885, so many people were downtown that "the line of hitching racks were crowded with animals and vehicles". Not that the crime rate had improved much, for in February of 1886, Ora McHenry had his .45 caliber Colt gun stolen, probably by a "burly porter" at a local hotel, Ross House.

Guest lists of those attending the many dances, musicals, theatricals, and parties at Rogers Hall, or the popular roller skating events at the skating rink, did not include the Robert McHenrys. Rather, they were mentioned among those present at weddings, such as the "nuptuals of Miss Elaine Brinkerhoff and Ira G. Hoag at the residence of the bride's parents" in February 1884, and their names occasionally appeared on private party lists. One which they attended in March 1886, hosted by Mr. and Mrs. J.F. Tucker, was typical. The guests began to arrive "at an early hour", and by 9 o'clock had well filled the larger double parlors. Cards and games were played until supper was annouced, when the group adjourned to the dining room where "a well laden table of toothsome delicacies was spread". Following the "much relished feast", entertainment was provided by vocal and instrumental musical selections, and the party ended sometime after midnight.

An important event for the Robert McHenrys was the marriage of their only child, Oramil, to Louise Bilicke on March 3, 1886. The ceremony took place at 11 o'clock in the morning at Modesto's most elegant hotel, Ross House, which was the home of the bride. Proprietor of the hotel was Louise's brother, Albert C. Bilicke, formerly of San Francisco, who, with his father, had come to Modesto in 1885 to take over the management of the hotel. Her parents were Mr. and Mrs. Charles Gustav Bilicke, and Bilicke, originally from Prussia, was a well known hotel man. Guests included the families and close friends, and the major gifts and their donors were listed in the newspaper. This article is especially interesting and is reproduced in Appendix A. Note that the Robert McHenrys' gift was "a handsome double case of silver table and tea spoons". The bride and groom honeymooned in San Francisco before returning to live at the Bald Eagle Ranch.

The custom of receiving callers on New Year's Day was continued by Mrs. Robert McHenry on January 1, 1887, except that on this occasion she was assisted by her new daughter-in-law, Mrs. Ora McHenry. The hours were from 12 to 9 p.m.

There were many life-threatening hazards in the 1880s, one of which had to do with runaway horses. On January 7, 1887, a couple was riding in their carriage near 15th and I Streets when the horses became frightened and started to run. As the carriage rounded the corner by the residence of Mr. and Mrs. Robert McHenry, the buggy was upset, discharging the occupants. Both were reported as being "insensible" by the neighbors who came to their rescue. Frequent runaways were

The skating rink is affording numerous hearty laughs for the inhabitants of Modesto. Several of the impressions taken on the floor last evening could be plainly seen this morning.

STANISLAUS COUNTY NEWS
April 17, 1885

The Latest Wedding Kink

Throwing the bridal bouquet, is an exciting feature of modern weddings. Before leaving home, the bride tosses her bridal flowers into the air, and the maiden who is lucky enough to catch it as it falls, will, if the fates know what they are about and conduct things properly, be the next to wed. We have not learned who was the lucky catcher at the McHenry-Bilicke wedding.

STANISLAUS COUNTY NEWS
March 5, 1886

common in town, sometimes involving large teams of five or six horses or mules.

About this time, grocer A. Minotti proclaimed that "groceries were cheaper than ever before" such as: lettuce, 25 cents a dozen; choice cauliflower, $1 a dozen; cabbage 1½ cents a pound; artichokes, 25 cents a dozen; butter, 50 cents a roll; California cream cheese, 12½ cents a pound; fairly good flour, $3.75 a barrel; best in the world flour, $5.25 a barrel; good green coffee, $1 for 9 pounds; and best ground coffee in town, 15 cents a pound.

The Bald Eagle Ranch had a good wheat crop in 1887, judging by a glowing May report that described the stalks in some places as five feet high, with full ears of grain.

Robert McHenry, and later his son Oramil, were two of the handful of foresighted men in this county who fought the long, and often discouraging, battle for irrigation. By 1886, as the demand for wheat was diminishing, frequent periods of drought meant sudden poverty for many farmers, especially those with smaller acreages. Finally, in 1887 a bill called the Wright Irrigation Act, sponsored by Stanislaus County Assemblyman C.C Wright, was passed by the state legislature. It allowed for the creation of local irrigation districts that would be owned, financed, and managed by the people. Immediately, both Modesto and Turlock organized their districts. The Modesto Irrigation District was formed at an election held June 9, 1887, at which time Robert McHenry, running unopposed, was elected director for District 3. The Irrigation District Board of Directors held its first organizational meeting at the First National Bank on July 23, and he was elected president of the Board, a post he held until almost the end of his life. According to the *Modesto Irrigation District Record of Minutes* for July 30, 1887, Robert McHenry and J.W. Davison were chosen to communicate with engineers for the surveying of the first canal, and he was also elected to a committee to discuss the building of a dam on the Tuolumne River with the Turlock Irrigation District. On April 4, 1888, he was reelected to the post of Modesto Irrigation District Director for District 3. Records of M.I.D. minutes show that Robert attended many meetings, often weekly, and actively participated in the development of the water system that eventually would lead to the prosperity of the Modesto region.

Meanwhile, in October 1887, the Turlock Irrigation District was created by a vote of the people, and that Board offered $50,000 worth of bonds for sale to begin the financing of its project. When the sealed bids were opened on November 7, Robert McHenry was the only bidder. His bid was $45,000.

The period from 1887 into mid-1888 was filled with meetings for Robert McHenry. He was president of the Board of Trade which at times met every week, as well as treasurer of the Stanislaus County Pioneer Society. The banks with which he was associated met frequently, and he participated in Republican political activities.

On the night of October 18, 1887, Robert chaired a meeting of the Board of Trade at Rogers Hall, during which he reported that the expense of the County's display at the State Fair had been $489. This meeting is also of special interest because it occurred on the same date as the birth of Robert's first grandchild. The birth notice in the *Stanislaus Weekly News* read, "McHENRY -- at Modesto, October 18,

1887, to the wife of Ora McHenry, a son -- 11 pounds". He was named Robert Albert.

An item dated December 16, 1887, noted that "the six weeks old son of Mr. and Mrs. Ora McHenry, whose life has been despaired of the past few days, is reported somewhat better today". The McHenrys were fortunate in the survival of their son, for the infant mortality rate was very high at this time in Modesto. It seemed as though almost every family suffered an infant death, from a variety of diseases such as diptheria, scarlet fever, meningitis, consumption, congestion of the lungs, and pneumonia. Causes of death often were not even listed, probably because they were not known. Older children were also the frequent victims of all of the above mentioned ailments plus tuberculosis and whooping cough, as well as of accidents such as drownings, gunshot wounds, burns from kerosene lamps, fatal falls from horses and trees, and being kicked by mules and horses.

As 1887 came to a close, the town's streets were still muddy, following a dusty summer, and remained unlighted and littered with rubbish, no doubt affected by events such as the 2000 sheep that went through the town en route to Fresno in November. Although the City Board of Trustees enacted ordinances covering many of the town's problems, the implementation of these laws was expensive and difficult. There continued to be complaints about drunks on the streets, fighting in the saloons, and hobos in town. And on December 23 of that year, at 8:00 o'clock in the morning, all of the residents in the area of 10th and I Street gathered to watch an "exciting chase" of a jackrabbit by a greyhound dog.

In January of each year, Robert McHenry's banks held annual meetings of their stockholders and elected directors and officers. On January 13, 1888, when he was again reelected president and a director of the First National Bank of Modesto, it was noted that this bank was in an especially "flourishing" condition, having increased its capital to $100,000 from $50,000 since its formation in June of 1884. He was also renamed to the directorship of the Modesto Bank at its stockholders' meeting during the same month.

It was announced in July of 1888 that Robert McHenry was sick and confined to his home for several days. This was the beginning of what would become a progressively debilitating illness. According to news items, he went to the springs of Lake County for his health and, en route home in November, suffered a siege of "apoplexy" (stroke) and returned in a "precarious condition". His right side was paralyzed, and he became an invalid.

On December 23, 1888, his second grandson was born. The child of Ora and Louise, the baby's name was Albert Hewitt.

Ailing Robert McHenry was not present at the bank and M.I.D. meetings in 1889, and was replaced as a director of the Modesto Bank by his son Ora at the January meeting. Ora also was elected assistant cashier of the First National Bank, although his father remained as president. During this time, Robert's duties as president of the M.I.D. Board of Directors were fulfilled by A.G. Carver, chairman pro-tem, until Robert's resignation on July 17, 1889.

On Tuesday, June 24, 1890, at age 63, Robert McHenry died at his I Street home, where his funeral was held the following Thursday at 2 P.M. The newspaper account of the funeral is reproduced in Appendix B, and you will note that the "large parlors were crowded". The service was read by Rev. Henry C. Gillingham of the Presbyterian Church, and the funeral procession was one of Modesto's biggest.

ROBERT McHENRY, THE MAN

It isn't easy to assess the personality and character traits of a man a hundred years after his existence. Yet in the case of Robert McHenry, many clues exist to give us some idea of the kind of person he was and the values that he considered important. It is significant that, in this small village where life was often difficult, he managed to participate in a wide variety of activities and was a leader in practically everything he did. He was an officer, and often president or chairman, of almost every group he was affiliated with, including the banks, Irrigation District boards, operation of the schools, the Board of Trade, the Pioneer Society, and the church building committee. The *Stanislaus Weekly News* of July 16, 1887 painted a word-picture of Robert McHenry, by way of explaining that he had been unopposed in the first Irrigation District election because his popularity precluded the placing of an opponent against him. It described him as "a man always calm, thoughtful, and poised, with clear reasoning powers, with great capacity for business, with the best of financial standing". Finally, at the time of his death in 1890, a tribute in the same newspaper noted that he was associated with many community enterprises and that "he possessed great executive ability, and almost everything he became associated with prospered". It continued,

As a business man, Mr. McHenry was always loyal to the fixed and legitimate principles of commercial life. His word was his bond, and his judgment seldom failed. When he was persuaded that a person merited his consideration he was kind and sympathetic. And as one was heard to remark recently: 'A worthy man never appealed to him in vain'. Mr. McHenry was a man of few words, and his chief delight was the quiet of his home amidst his family. His death is a public loss.

BORN,

McHENRY - At Modesto, December 23, 1888, to the wife of Ora McHenry a son.

STANISLAUS COUNTY NEWS
December 28, 1888

Birth notice, Albert Hewitt McHenry

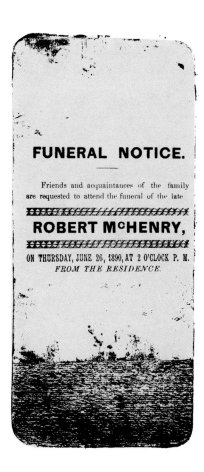

FUNERAL NOTICE.

Friends and acquaintances of the family are requested to attend the funeral of the late

XXXXXXXXXXXXXXXXXXXXX
ROBERT McHENRY,
XXXXXXXXXXXXXXXXXX
ON THURSDAY, JUNE 26, 1890, AT 2 O'CLOCK P. M.
FROM THE RESIDENCE.

Matilda McHenry.

CHAPTER 3

THE WORLD OF MATILDA McHENRY

THE QUIET YEARS

Matilda Margaret Hewitt McHenry apparently led a quiet, widow's life in the big house from the time of her husband's death in 1890 until her own passing in 1896. The number of servants needed to maintain the home is unknown, but her staff was probably similar to that of a later period which included a cook, maid, groom, and gardener. However, the newspapers of the day occasionally referred to a shortage of "domestics", which may have been a factor. Modesto's population had grown to about 2400, but the McHenry house was still at the edge of the town. The large Willis Bledsoe home on the northeasterly corner of 16th and I Streets, the two story Henry Voight house at 16th and J, and the Charles Bennett one story between I and J were all built in 1885. The Bennett property, which consisted of four lots at 909 16th Street, was located across the alley from the McHenry's orange grove. In the early 1890s, a nursery-floral business was operated on this site by Mrs. Anna Bennett, which continued for many years. Most of the other lots across from the McHenry home on both 15th and I Streets were probably still vacant, although some of them had been sold. For example, in October of 1890, the *Daily Evening News* reported that department store owner Peter Latz had purchased three lots between the Presbyterian Church and the McHenry resident on I Street for $1000, noting "The lots are among the most desirable in this city for a residence".

Matilda McHenry most likely maintained some contact with her three brothers and their families, who lived in Farmington and Stockton. One brother, James Rogers Hewitt, became well known in Modesto because of his frequent visits from his home in Stockton, during which he may have stayed at the McHenry house. And she presumably attended the Stockton wedding of another brother, William T. Hewitt, on October 8, 1891. Both of her sisters had died many years before, each leaving a widower and three young children. One sister, Sarah Ann Hewitt, had married Charles Henry Huffman of Merced, whose story is related in Chapter 2. Her other sister, Eliza Jane Hewitt, also married an interesting man, Henry Langworthy. In 1860, he founded a prosperous little town called Langworth (which Robert McHenry gave as his address when he became Clerk of the McHenry School District), the settlement that died out when the railroad went to nearby Oakdale in 1871. According to Matilda's niece, Ruth Hewitt Herbert (daughter of William Hewitt), Langworthy owned land in the Farmington area near where the Samuel Hewitt family camped during their first rainy winter in 1853. He later became the postmaster of Langworth. The three adult children of Eliza and Henry Langworthy were named as cousins receiving $1000 each under the terms of Ora McHenry's will in 1906. They were Ralph Langworthy and Mrs. W.W. Granger (Helen Langworthy), both of Fresno, and Mrs. A.W. Mercer (Mary Langworthy) of Chicago, Illinois. W.W. Granger was an early day Modesto pharmacist.

Matilda remained close to her church during these years and must have felt somewhat uncomfortable when she was called upon to testify against her minister in November of 1891. Charges had been filed against Rev. H.C. Gillingham of the First Presbyterian Church on a number of counts of misconduct, and a well attended trial lasting about a week was conducted at the church. Matilda McHenry and four other persons testified that the defendant had "told them at different times of the great wealth of his father", a story that apparently had been discredited. Rev. Gillingham was finally removed from his position on the basis of two of the charges, "using vulgar and indecent language, and lying".

Ora McHenry, Matilda's son, was very busy in the early 1890s, operating and expanding the businesses originated by his late father. In 1891, he built a new home on the Bald Eagle Ranch where he and his family resided, so it is not known how much time he spent at the town residence of his mother. However, she may on occasion have entertained her two grandsons, Robert (called Bob) and Albert, who would have stayed in bedrooms upstairs during visits. On October 17, 1891, Matilda McHenry became a third-time grandmother with the birth of Ora and Louise's daughter, Ora Louise, born in San Francisco.

The "McHenry Monument" in the Masonic (Acacia) Cemetery.

It was during this period, almost three years after the death of Robert McHenry, that the "McHenry Monument" arrived in Modesto. The Stanislaus Weekly News reported that, on February 24, 1893, the completed monument had been placed over the remains of Robert McHenry in the 20 by 20 foot family plot in the Masonic Cemetery. Cemetery records show that the gravesite, in lot 2, block 15 of the cemetery, had been purchased by Ora McHenry on June 25, 1890 for $40 in gold coin. The plot consisted of 10 gravesites, and Robert McHenry was placed in grave number 2. The monument had been specially designed and constructed by well known marble carver D.J. Spellman of Stockton, made of granite produced in the granite works at Barre, Vermont. The total weight of the sarcophagus was 18 tons, with a height of 8 feet and dimensions of 9 by 5½ feet. The entire surface was covered with marble slabs, and the design was described as having plaster corners, carved caps, and mouldings of Grecian design. Proclaimed as "one of the most attractive and noticeable monuments in the cemetery" it was designed so that slabs could be removed when necessary for other family members. This monument still stands today in the Masonic (Acacia) Cemetery on Scenic Drive, where six of the ten graves are occupied by McHenrys.

On March 3, 1893, Matilda McHenry attended a dinner party given by Mr. and Mrs. Ora McHenry in their "elegant home" at the Bald Eagle Ranch to commemorate their seventh anniversary. "At 6 o'clock covers were spread for ten persons and one of the most appetizing and delicious of dinners was served, after which a season was devoted to musical selections and social converse", the *News* said. Guests were Mrs. C.G. Bilicke (Louise McHenry's mother), Mrs. Matilda McHenry, Mrs. E.A. Head of San Francisco, Mr. and Mrs. George Stoddard, W.H. Hatton, P.H. Griffin, and J.H. Maddrill.

May of 1893 found Matilda, her son Ora, and his wife Louise attending the World's Fair in Chicago. They were gone for several weeks and also visited other Eastern locations.

Matilda became a grandmother for the fourth time on May 26, 1895 with the birth of Ora's fourth child, named Russell.

A revealing incident was reported in June 1895, when a "valuable driving horse" owned by Ora McHenry died in the stable at his mother's home. The horse had gotten out of its stall during the night and "into the wheat used for the chicken feed". The animal gorged itself, which caused its death the next morning. This story indicates two things: one, that Ora McHenry kept at least one horse in the stables at the McHenry house, and two, that chickens also resided at 15th and I Streets in 1895.

January and February of 1896 were tragic months for the McHenry family. On January 15, Russell McHenry, aged 7 months and 19 days, died at the Bald Eagle Ranch. The funeral services were held on January 24 at the ranch and were private. Less than four weeks later, it was reported that Matilda McHenry was suffering from pneumonia. Following an illness of just a few days, she died at her home on Friday, February 28, 1896, at age 57. Again, the parlors of the McHenry Mansion were the scene of a funeral, held the following Sunday at 2 o'clock, with an unusually large gathering of friends and relatives. She was buried beside her husband in the McHenry plot. The newspaper account of Matilda McHenry's passing is of interest and is reproduced in Appendix C.

On May 15, 1896, in the Superior Court, Ora McHenry was appointed executor of his mother's estate. Her will left all of the estate including the home to her son, except for two bequests to her church. One was in the amount of $5000, to be placed in a fund for the erection of a new Presbyterian church building, and $10,000 was to be placed in a permanent trust and "loaned" (or invested), with the interest going to pay for ministers' salaries. The money apparently was put to good use, because eight years later, on March 27, 1904, during the 25th anniversary ceremonies held at the church, Mrs. B.F. Surryhne read an historical sketch in which she said,

> In the spring of 1896, upon the death of Mrs. Matilda McHenry, this church received a bequest of $15,000, the income from which has enabled the First Presbyterian Church of Modesto to be maintained without Board assistance through the years of financial depression that have intervened.

The 1880 church building was torn down in 1910 and a new one immediately constructed on the same site, in part financed by Matilda's money.

C.G. Bilicke and wife, of Los Angeles, M.H. Huffman and wife of Merced, C.H. Huffman and wife of San Francisco, and Mrs. W.W. Granger of Fresno, were in Modesto yesterday to attend the funeral of the late Mrs. Matilda M. McHenry.

MODESTO DAILY EVENING NEWS
March 2, 1896

Ora McHenry.

CHAPTER 4

THE WORLD OF ORAMIL McHENRY

THE EARLY YEARS, 1861-1890

Oramil McHenry, called Ora by friends and family, was raised during an era when many Modestans danced until dawn, attended masquerade balls and surprise parties, and roller skated at the rink. In 1880, at age 19, he was the partner of Miss Minnie Hurd at the town's first leap year party. "Rogers Hall was ablaze for the occasion. Never in its history was it so beautiful", claimed the March 19 issue of the *Stanislaus Weekly News*. At ten past 10 o'clock, the Grand March was called, and over sixty couples filed around the wall. "No such a sight had ever been seen in Modesto before. The brilliant costumes of the ladies as they marched and countermarched under the gas light produced an effect that was charming beyond description". A four piece orchestra provided the music for a program of dances that included the waltz, schottische, quadrille, and polka. At 1 a.m., a supper was served at the nearby Prentiss Hotel, after which dancing was resumed until a late hour -- so late that, "as the familiar strains of *Home Sweet Home* fell like a benison upon the ears of the revelers, the gray streaks of dawn shot over the Sierras and lit up, with their faint light, the eastern heavens".

On another occasion, the following year, young Ora was among those present at one of Modesto's famous masquerade balls, also held at Rogers Hall, for which he was dressed as a prince. Over 150 persons were masked and costumed, with another 150 uncostumed. Dancing to a small orchestra occupied the evening.

A surprise party was hosted by Ora McHenry in March of 1884, at the family's Bald Eagle Ranch. Dancing continued without interruption until a late hour when a "splendid supper which had been provided by the ladies was served. After supper, the party turned into a leap year dance and the ladies acquitted themselves with honor in their new role". The party adjourned at 4 o'clock, according to the *Stanislaus News*.

Ora was undoubtedly much more socially inclined than his father, but he was also a hard worker. He was educated at the McHenry District School and lived at the Bald Eagle Ranch until 1879, when he was 18 and the family probably moved into town. He took a three year course at the University of California, only a few years after its founding in 1869. Then he returned to become bookkeeper at the First National Bank, of which his father was president.

It isn't known when he first became acquainted with Louise Bilicke, but she didn't arrive in town until perhaps January of 1885. That was when her father, hotel man Charles G. Bilicke, and brother, Albert C. Bilicke, leased the Ross House Hotel for three years, with an option for five. Albert had previously managed the Cosmopolitan Hotel at Tombstone, Arizona. All newspaper advertisements listed Albert as the proprietor of Ross House, although the father was also involved in the managment, at least until 1887 when he acquired a hotel at Dunsmuir, California. It is interesting that on New Year's Day of 1886, while Mr. and Mrs. Robert McHenry were receiving callers at

Young Ora McHenry.

their home, Louise Bilicke was also entertaining at an open house with three other young women in the handsomely decorated parlors of Ross House, where she lived.

Ora McHenry and Louise Emma Bilicke were married on March 3, 1886, as described in Chapter 2 and Appendix A. He was 25 years of age, and she was almost 19. Following a San Francisco honeymoon, they settled on the Bald Eagle Ranch, just as Ora's parents had when they were newlyweds in 1859. For a few months following the wedding, there were occasional reports indicating that Mr. and Mrs. Ora McHenry, of the Bald Eagle Ranch, were in town.

Yosemite was a favorite vacation spot for Modestans, and on June 11, 1886, Ora McHenry and Albert Bilicke, Louise's brother, went camping in Yosemite, returning in about a week. Bilicke's Ross House was by now becoming a social center and, according to an expansive Bilicke, was the "only first class hotel between Los Angeles and San Francisco". It had been extensively remodeled and had a dining room large enough to seat 100. The names and hometowns of those registered frequently appeared in the newspapers, with entries from Chinese Camp, Coulterville, Fresno, Galt, Knights Ferry, La Grange, Merced, Oakland, Sacramento, San Francisco, Snelling, Stockton, and Turlock.

In the early years, Modesto's Fourth of July celebrations were boisterous and joyous. Everyone participated, including Ora McHenry who, on July 4, 1886, served as a Marshall's Aide and successfully helped to maintain law and order during the day's festivities.

Ora's and Louise's two sons were born 14 months apart, Robert Albert (nicknamed Bob) on Friday, October 23, 1887, and Albert Hewitt on December 23, 1888, both at the Bald Eagle Ranch.

By the beginning of 1889, Ora was taking over his infirmed father's responsibilities. In January, he replaced Robert McHenry as a director of the Modesto Bank and was named assistant cashier of the First National Bank. Undoubtedly, he also was managing the operations of the Bald Eagle Ranch. On July 3, 1890, just ten days after the death of his father, Ora was elected president and a director of the First National Bank at a meeting of the stockholders. Vice president was W.R. Wood, and J.E. Ward was cashier. The *Stanislaus Weekly News* commented that, with one exception, Ora McHenry, at age 29, was the youngest bank president in the United States.

Now, with the death of Robert McHenry, son Ora took over the reigns of the McHenry banking and agricultural empire, which represented some of the most successful business operations of the county.

THE PRODUCTIVE YEARS, 1890-1902

Ora McHenry was a progressive farmer, and he immediately expanded the Bald Eagle Ranch into new areas of agricultural development. In September 1890, he and his ranch foreman went to Fresno to investigate the "modus operandi of preparing and cultivating soil for raisins and fruit growing". By the following February, it was announced that he had just planted 160 acres of fruit trees on the upland of the Bald Eagle Ranch, and 30 acres of vines, and that the ranch already had 100 acres of prunes, 40 acres of White Adriatic figs, and 10 acres each of white nectarines and French apricots.

Local politics was spirited and partisan in Modesto's early years, and when Ora entered the November 4, 1890 election for Supervisor, Fourth District, it was as a Republican. He ran against incumbent Democrat G.W. Toombs and was defeated by 21 votes out of the 520 cast. Democrats dominated the local political scene for many years, although the California governorship was won by Republican Henry Markham. On the national scene, Grover Cleveland had become unpopular by the 1888 election and was defeated by Republican Benjamin Harrison.

1891 was another busy year for Ora McHenry. In January, he made news by installing a telephone line between his ranch and the bank in Modesto, one of the first in the community. He also took train trips to Stockton and San Francisco, including one in May with his wife. McHenry house guests included Louise's parents, the Bilickes from Dunsmuir, and Mrs. Paul Wickersham, wife of one of the editors of the *San Francisco Examiner*. Then, on August 7, 1891, a news item announced that the foundation was being prepared for the construction of Ora McHenry's "handsome two story residence on the Bald Eagle Ranch". A week later a load of lumber arrived for the residence, an impressive Queen Anne Victorian home that still stands on Crawford Road, about six miles north of Modesto. It is of interest that, unlike the McHenry Mansion which was built using architectural drawings prepared by a Stockton architect, the plans for the Bald Eagle house came from a mail-order catalogue of house designs, a common practice at that time. The plan was design #36 in *The Cottage Souvenir, No. 2*, subtitled *A Repository of Artistic Architecture, Miscellaneous Designs*, by architect George Franklin Barber. The book was copyright 1890 in Knoxville, Tennessee, and the cost of full working drawings for design #36 was $55. Eric and Mary Christopherson, who purchased the house in 1972, are in possession of a copy of the book and also a testimonial letter written to the book company by Ora McHenry in April 1892, as follows:

> Modesto Cal
> April 18, 1892
> Dear Sirs: Yours received, and in reply will state that the contractor stated that my plans and specifications were the most complete and accurate that he had ever worked from.
>
> Yours respectfully,
> O. McHenry,
> President, First National Bank, Modesto

Perhaps one incentive for building the new house was the anticipated arrival of a third child, who was born in San Francisco on October 17, 1891. She was named Ora Louise.

The Ora McHenry's new home at the Bald Eagle Ranch.

Ora's business interests continued to prosper. In October 1891, he became the treasurer and a director of a group calling itself the Stanislaus Development Company. And the January 1892 annual report of the First National Bank showed that it was "flourishing", with $5000 added to the capital of the Union Savings Bank, the adjunct bank under the same ownership.

During this period, Ora McHenry was a volunteer fireman, serving as a member of the Modesto Fire Department's Hose Company. This was probably risky, since fires in Modesto were common in the 1890s. Also, life in the community was not especially safe, according to a report from the State Board of Health issued in January 1892. It stated that Modesto's 153 deaths the previous year represented an unusually high death rate, which local officials immediately disputed. House and business burglaries were on the increase, and reports of local divorces and suicides had become routine. Grocery prices were similar to those in the 1880s, even though the country was now heading into a financial depression. It lasted for several years, through the second presidential term of Grover Cleveland, who had defeated Benjamin Harrison in 1892. $1.00 bought 5 pounds of choice coffee or 14 pounds of granulated sugar at I.E. Gilbert's store, with flour advertised at $3.65 a barrel, 20 bars of laundry soap for 40 cents, 50 ounces of baking powder at 45 cents, and tobacco per plug, 40 cents. Excursion one-way train fares were $4.15 to San Francisco, $5.40 to Santa Cruz, $3.50 to Sacramento, and $1.30 to Stockton, with reductions for round trips.

In January of 1893, Ora again made a try for political office, becoming a candidate for treasurer of the Modesto Irrigation District. Three men were in the race, and J.W. Davison was the winner. Davison had served as secretary, with Robert McHenry as president, of the first M.I.D. Board in 1887. Ora continued his whole-hearted support of the irrigation movement, giving generously of both his money and time to its cause. A group of anti-irrigationists, calling themselves the Defense Association, had vigorously fought against irrigation from the beginning, mainly based on their fear of increased taxes, but also because some didn't wish to change their methods of farming and even considered the irrigation plan unworkable. Despite their continuing opposition, the Modesto and Turlock Irrigation Districts joined together and succeeded in building La Grange Dam to provide water for both districts. Completed in 1893, at a cost of $543,000, it was considered an engineering masterpiece for its time. Unfortunately, by the time the dam was constructed and the main canals had been dug, the money had run out with much of the project yet to be completed. The next few years were marked by law suits and court battles, and only the donations of private funds by citizens such as Ora McHenry kept the project alive.

Life was not all work for Ora McHenry. In the spring of 1893, special excursion train fares to the Chicago Worlds Fair were being advertised, which perhaps Ora, wife Louise, and his mother Matilda took advantage of when they traveled East to the Fair in May. And in March of 1893, and again the following year, the McHenrys celebrated their March 4 wedding anniversary by entertaining in their home at the Bald Eagle Ranch. The first was described in Chapter 3, which included Matilda McHenry as a guest, and the second, observing eight years of marriage, was a Sunday afternoon party. The dinner of "all the choicest viands", lasting some two hours, was followed by singing and "social converse".

In the spring and summer of 1893, Modesto's dirt streets were reported to be dustier than ever before, due to the digging of ditches for the installation of water and sewer pipes. This was the result of a successful bond election held in November 1892, for $60,000 worth of water bonds and $25,000 in sewer bonds. The Modesto City Water Works, which absorbed and expanded the town's original water company, was completed in October 1893, and hook-ups to the new system began immediately. It can be assumed that the McHenry house was among those connecting into the city's water system at about this time. The Modesto City Board of Trustees established rules for making such connections, including the requirement that only one inch pipe could be used, that no person could have more than one connection for every two lots or 50 feet, and that all connections to tanks and windmills were to be discontinued. A long list of monthly water charges was issued by the Trustees, several of which would have applied to the McHenrys, such as $1 for one private water closet and 50 cents for each additional on the same premises; 58 cents for bathtubs used in private dwellings; $1.15 for garden watering for each 25 by 140 foot lot and any greater area charged at the same rate; and 50 cents for private stables with one horse and buggy, plus 50 cents for each additional horse and carriage. Many stores were placed on water meters, and failure to adhere to regulations concerning specified watering hours resulted in fines and disconnection of water services.

It was during this same period, in around 1894, that the McHenry house probably also hooked into the city's newly constructed sewer system, which dumped the town's raw sewage into the Tuolumne River. Another city service that would have affected the McHenrys was the installation of a gas street lamp at the corner of 15th and I Streets, which occurred in 1895. In that same year, Ora McHenry appeared before the City Board of Trustees to request a telephone right of way on I Street or J Street. The petition was granted for J Street, so a telephone apparently was installed in the McHenry Mansion in 1895. However, the important utility of electricity for the house had to wait at least nine more years, when the city finally adopted a system at the end of 1903.

Meanwhile, back at the ranch, in August of 1894 Ora McHenry journeyed to Fresno to meet with an architect concerning plans for building a raisin dryhouse, which would be modeled after one used at the Lucerne Vineyard at Hanford. This is significant, because it marked the further expansion of the McHenry ranch operations into the processing and shipping of raisins. The raisin dryer was soon built, with dimensions of 50 x 120 feet and a capacity of 75 tons of raisin grapes, which would make 25 tons of raisins. A 50 x 180 foot two story packing house was also constructed, immediately adjoining the dryer. The cost of both structures was $25,000.

Surprise parties were very popular in early Modesto, although it appeared that few of those honored were ever really surprised. On Saturday evening, September 15, 1894, a merry group made the trip from town to the Bald Eagle Ranch, which reportedly took up to an hour by carriage, to surprise Mr. and Mrs. Ora McHenry. The result was amusing.

> Upon arriving at the handsome home of the recipients, it was found that they had anticipated the "surprise" and had made extensive arrangements for their reception, both in the residence and in the packing house adjoining. In the latter, a portion of the upstairs department was festooned with evergreens, flowers, fruits, and the national colors.

Dancing and singing were followed by a late, "splendid" supper.

A fourth McHenry child was born at the Bald Eagle Ranch on May 26, 1895, a boy who was named Russell.

Summers in Modesto were quiet socially, with many of the families escaping from the heat and the mosquitos by spending time at the seashore. A special $4.00 train fare to Santa Cruz was announced in June 1895, but the McHenrys chose to spend their three week vacation at Lake Tahoe in August. When they returned, they were visited by Louise's parents, the Bilickes, who by now had left Dunsmuir for Los Angeles. Brother Albert was also an occasional visitor, having given up Ross House by 1891 and acquired a hotel in Santa Cruz. He later located in Southern California.

Another party hosted by the McHenrys at the Bald Eagle Ranch was held in the upper story of the packing house on Friday, September 20, 1895, where a portion of the large room was turned into a ballroom, decorated with evergreens. The grand march was played shortly after

9 p.m. to music played by Professors Hintze, Stevens and Cook. Dancing by the 120 persons present continued until midnight when a basket supper was served, followed by more dancing until early in the morning. During the event, the guests toured the packing house dryer with their host and the plant superintendent and, according to the *Stanislaus Weekly News*, were shown "all the details of the large company, many of whom had never seen anything of the kind before". Then, just a few hours later, at 11 a.m. on Saturday, Ora McHenry received a telephone call at the First National Bank in town informing him that the packing house was in flames. The straw used to fire the large engine in the plant had ignited, but by the time he could get to the scene, on horseback or by carriage, 60 employees had already put out the fire using two heavy streams of water. At the time, the 75 ton capacity dryer was almost full of raisin grapes, for drying and curing, and there was also $10,000 worth of seedwheat, barley, and other articles stored in the building. The successful fire fighting operation was attributed to the "splendid fire facilities" at the ranch and the presence of mind of the employees. It is of interest that 16 years later, in July 1911, the packing shed and a number of other buildings at the Bald Eagle Ranch were completely destoryed by fire (see Chapter Notes, page 111).

Tragedy struck the McHenry family in 1896. On January 15, six and a half month old Russell McHenry died at the Bald Eagle Ranch, following a three week illness. "The child was a remarkably bright little fellow and was the joy of the household", said the *Stanislaus News*. Then, in less than two months, on February 28, Ora's mother, Matilda McHenry, died of pneumonia at her home on I Street (see Chapter 3 and Appendix C). And on December 6 of the same year, Louise's father, Charles G. Bilicke, succumbed from cancer in Los Angeles.

Modesto's population of around 2,400 was not increasing at this time, principally because the development of irrigation had become stalled. However, conditions in the town were gradually improving. The streets were now being dampened by two sprinkling carts working 15 hours a day, one for five hours and the other for ten hours, pulled by four horses. The number of gas street lamps was increasing, and in 1896 the Board of Trustees accepted a bid from the Modesto Gas Company of $3.00 per month per lamp. They also decided to continue with gas as the source of power for city lighting because it was so much less expensive than electricity. An ordinance was passed forbidding the keeping of any swine or more than two cows within the city, and speed limits were established for bicycles and tricycles of eight miles an hour on the streets and six miles per hour on sidewalks. The runaway horse problem was still acute, with many wagon and buggy accidents reported downtown. Fire was a continuing concern, and the Ross House burned down in 1897. Meyer and Latz store on 10th Street advertised ladies' muslin drawers for 25 cents, low cut shoes 50 cents, and hand made men's suits for $13 up. Squirrels and jackrabbits were considered major pests, and the Board

Louise Bilicke.

Dance at the Bald Eagle.

One of the largest and most successful dancing parties that has ever been given in this county was that held at the McHenry packing house, on the Bald Eagle ranch, last evening. Fully 150 ladies and gentlemen were present and all who attended had a most enjoyable time. The music was furnished by Fallon and Staurt, of Modesto, and Quinn and Beasley of Stockton. It was excellent. Dancing was indulged in in the upper room of the handsome packing house and supper was served on the lower floor.

STANISLAUS COUNTY WEEKLY NEWS
April 23, 1898

DIED.

McHENRY — At Bald Eagle ranch, near Modesto, January 15, 1896, Russell, son of Mr. and Mrs. O. McHenry, aged 6 months and 19 days.

STANISLAUS COUNTY WEEKLY NEWS
January 17, 1896

Death notice, Russell McHenry

of Supervisors passed a squirrel and rabbit bounty ordinance, giving two cents for an entire squirrel tail or rabbit scalp including both ears. Rabbit drives were frequent occurrences, resulting in the extermination of thousands of jackrabbits at a time.

Ora McHenry was the sole heir to his Mother's $206,069 estate, with the exception of her bequest to the Presbyterian Church (see Chapter 3), and also inherited the Mansion on I Street. It is not known exactly when he and his family moved into town from the Bald Eagle Ranch, but the children ultimately were enrolled in the Modesto school at 14th and I Streets, sometimes called the Brick School House, just a block from their home.

It is fascinating to think about the McHenry Mansion as a functioning home for a growing family consisting of father, mother, three children, and frequent visitors. Uses of the downstairs rooms probably remained the same as during the Robert McHenry era, with the double parlors opened up for large formal entertaining, the front parlor reserved for guests, the back parlor and library used by the family, the front corner room utilized as an office, and meals served in the dining room. But, except for the sitting room and the master bedroom, the upstairs room arrangement would have differed in Ora's era because of the needs of the children. One or two rooms at the rear of the house were probably used by the boys, with the front north corner bedroom possibly occupied by little Ora Louise. The staff of servants may have included a governess for the children as well as a cook,

Family Portrait: Oramil, Louise, Ora Louise, Albert, and Robert McHenry.

46

maid, gardener, and groomsman or carriage driver. They were housed either in the basement or quarters above the kitchen or in both. Certainly, the image of many children playing in the mansion is a pleasant one, which occurred one October Saturday afternoon when a children's birthday party was given in the house. The honorees were Miss Ora Louise and Master Robert McHenry, and 35 children played games and enjoyed refreshments especially prepared to "give joy to juvenile appetites", according to the *Daily Evening News.*

The last years of the 1890s were active ones for Ora McHenry. His expansion of the Bald Eagle Ranch was very successful and was described in an article about Modesto published in the *San Francisco Chronicle* on February 28, 1896. Devoting several paragraphs to the "enterprising banker, Ora McHenry, whose Bald Eagle ranch is an object lesson of what may yet be done all over this wonderful valley", the *Chronicle* stated that Ora "had sense enough to try diversified farming on a wide scale and his ranch is today a marvelous example of what may be done when farmers learn that the era of great fortunes in wheat are over". Then, in a direct interview that revealed Ora's optimistic philosophy, he was quoted as saying,

> I have 300 acres in orchard, and the experiment of five years past convinces me that Stanislaus County and Modesto have a future, even if wheat should be driven entirely from the list of paying products. Everything grows here successfully. I have 100 acres in prunes, 20 in apricots, 40 in white Adriatic figs, 40 in Tokay grapes, and 160 in Muscat. This is one of the greatest apricot soils in the world, and when we get water all over the county new blood will come here -- men with money, industry and ideas. Every county like this needs new and thrifty people.

Citing the need for irrigation in the Valley, the *Chronicle* then noted that the "great McHenry ranch could not be conducted but for centrifugal pumps which bring water from a depth of ninety feet". The article also discussed the McHenry hog raising operations, stating, "This thrifty young banker and rancher has made thousands of dollars out of hogs. He has his own packing houses and he buys more hogs than any man in the entire valley".

Ora was doing other things besides ranching and banking. He was part of a group formed to promote the building of a standard gauge steam railroad into Yosemite Valley. He also served on a committee appointed by the City Board of Trustees to devise ways and means of acquiring for Modesto a terminal of the Yosemite Valley and Merced Railway Company. He was a charter member of the Modesto Athletic Association, which later secured Wood and Turner's Hall for instruction in "club, dumb-bell and wand exercises". He served on the Republican's county auditing and credential committees, was a delegate to the Republican Assembly District convention, and participated in the reactivation of the Board of Trade, later representing that group at a convention in Porterville. In 1897 he went to San Francisco to make arrangements for the passage of three Modesto men to Alaska, one of whom was the harness maker at the Ranch. This was the time of the great rush to the Klondike Gold Fields, and the

STANISLAUS COUNTY WEEKLY NEWS Advertisement appearing frequently in late 1895 and early 1896.

newspapers frequently featured letters from local adventurers relating tales of severe hardship in their quest for riches. It was also the period of the Spanish American War, which occurred during the administration of William McKinley (1897-1901). In 1898 Ora built a large, two story brick building covering a quarter block on the northeasterly corner of 10th and I Street, replacing a burned-out wooden structure on the site that he had originally purchased in 1890. The building was modern for its day, with a plate glass front, and was occupied on the I Street side by I.E. Gilbert & Company's general store, Tucker & Perley stationers, and G.W. Elsey & Company's furniture store. *The Modesto Herald* newspaper had the 10th Street frontage around the corner, while upstairs, Dr. C.W. Evans had nine rooms, with Gilbert's store occupying the remainder. A year later Ora was involved in the organization of the Germania Oil Company, becoming its first president and a member of the Board of Directors. The company purchased land in Kings County for oil exploration and sold $20,000 worth of stock at $1 a share.

During this period, several large parties were given in the packing shed of the Bald Eagle Ranch, utilizing the top floor for dancing and the lower part for dining, with as many as 150 in attendance. One, in April of 1899, was especially festive, with the dining room gas lighted and a five piece orchestra playing for dancing until 4 a.m.

By 1899, Modesto had not had a Fourth of July celebration for seven years. During an April planning meeting held at the First National Bank, a large and enthusiastic group chose Ora McHenry to be chairman of the 1899 Fourth of July committee. The result, according to a news item, was the "grandest celebration ever witnessed in Modesto", which was complete in every detail with neither "hitch nor jar" in the whole day's festivities. In the early morning, handsomely decorated carriages were seen wending their way into town from all parts of the county, although the events did not really get underway until the cannon boomed out the national salute at 7 a.m. The businesses and residences were magnificently decorated, making Modesto "as attractive and pretty a little city as it was possible". The day included many kinds of sports competitions such as bicycle, wool sack, fat man's, donkey, greased pig, and hurdle races, a tennis tournament, baseball game, tug-of-war, a large parade featuring elaborate floats and marching bands, an open air band concert at the Courthouse Park from 4 to 6 p.m., a fireworks display set off at the railroad reservation after dark, and the Grand Ball held at Rogers Hall that night. Besides being general chairman and an exofficio member of all sub-committees, Ora McHenry also headed the auditing committee, a job that he frequently seemed to acquire, presumably due to his banking skills.

The Bald Eagle Ranch sold butchered beef and pork at markets in Oakdale and Modesto. Meat was also sold at the Ranch, according to local rancher Mae Giovanetti whose father owned property near the Bald Eagle and was a frequent customer. An accident occurring in July 1899 illustrates the presence of Bald Eagle Ranch butcher wagons in Modesto. One was parked in the alley behind the Tynan Hotel, between 9th and 10th Streets, while the driver was attending to a

View of Modesto, taken from the court-house in about 1895. Note the McHenry house and the Presbyterian Church on the left and the 14th Street School in the center of the picture.

customer. Suddenly, the horses started to run. First they hit a telephone pole on I Street, knocking off a wagon wheel, and then collided with a scavenger cart on 10th Street. The horses pulling the cart were injured and the butcher wagon was completely demolished. By now the wagon's harness had been broken, and the Bald Eagle horses continued their run until they were finally caught near the County Hospital.

In the spring of 1900, the G.P. Schafer Company opened its doors on the corner of 10th and I Streets. Located in the building that Ora McHenry built in 1898, it took over the business of I.E. Gilbert and Sons. The store was largely owned by Ora and was managed by his brother-in-law, George Schafer, who was married to Myrtie's sister, Matilda Conneau. Schafers sold a wide variety of merchandise and eventually became the largest mercantile establishment in the central valley. It remained in business until 1927.

The first half of 1901 was another difficult period for the McHenrys. Ora had just returned from a six week trip to Arizona, where he had purchased 1180 head of Hereford cattle to be shipped by special train to Oakdale, when on March 29 the announcement of his divorce from Louise appeared in the newspapers. Typical of the times, the settlement was described, giving Louise a yearly allowance of $2,100, with $600 a year child support for nine year old daughter Ora Louise. Louise and Ora Louise left immediately for Los Angeles, where they moved into the Hollenbeck Hotel, owned by her brother, Albert Bilicke. Ora remained at the McHenry house with his two sons, who by now were 12 and 13 years of age and in the fourth and sixth grades at the 14th Street School. It was just three months later, on June 30, that daughter Ora Louise died as a result of burns received during a fire caused from the igniting of an alcohol lamp in her room at the hotel. Her remains were returned to Modesto and buried in the family plot in the Masonic Cemetery.

Ora Louise McHenry was nine when she died from burns in July 1901.

49

One other noteworthy event occurred in the summer of 1901. Young Myrtie Conneau, originally from Modesto and a product of local schools, returned to her home town to teach. She had just graduated from Stanford University, in the class of '01 with an A.B. in history, and had been hired as the new teacher at the McHenry District School. By now, the school had about 35 students and included grades one through eight.

An interesting news item in the *Daily Evening News*, dated September 2, 1901, noted that Ora McHenry, his two sons Robert and Albert, and Miss Myrtie Conneau had returned from a month's trip East. They traveled on the Northern Pacific Railroad to Minneapolis and then west to "Chicago, Buffalo, Montreal, Canada, and the Thousand Islands in the St. Lawrence River, thence through the lakes and the Hudson River to New York City, to Saratoga and Philadelphia and home via St. Louis on the Santa Fe Railway". Family members have stated that Myrtie was a tutor for the McHenry boys during this period. She returned to her new job teaching in the McHenry District School, and Ora resumed his busy life of rancher-banker including business trips to San Francisco and Stockton, Board of Trade meetings, and an October bird hunting expedition in the Coast Range mountains with ten other men.

In November 1901, Myrtie Conneau participated in a three day Teacher's Institute held at the I.O.O.F. (Odd Fellows) Hall in Modesto and contributed to a discussion of "To What Extent Does the Modern Beautiful Primary Reader Affect The Reading Habits of the Children in Later Life?".

Ora's banking career continued to flourish, especially in early 1902 when it was announced that he had purchased 341 shares of Modesto Bank stock from the Cressey family. *The Daily News* refuted the "street rumor" that this would give him control of the bank, noting that his holdings were then only 650 shares out of the total of 2500 shares.

The struggle for irrigation, so bitterly fought during the 1890s, continued into the new century. After years of litigation and law suits, the anti-irrigationists achieved a majority on the Board of Directors of the Modesto Irrigation District in the election of 1899. This brought the project to a halt until 1901 when the opponents made a crucial mistake. They refused to call an election for officers of the M.I.D. A group of pro-irrigationists, including Ora McHenry, took them to court over this issue and won a decision, forcing an election. This time, all but one of the newly elected Board members were irrigationists, and the project was back on track. Much of the work previously accomplished had deteriorated, so it took two years to repair the damage and construct the new canals. However, in late 1903, the first water trickled onto the land of three farmers, one of whom was Ora McHenry. By the 1904 growing season, the irrigation system was ready to go.

THE LIVELY YEARS, 1902-1905

The next three years of Ora McHenry's life were very fruitful. It was also a time of renaissance for the McHenry Mansion. This period began on Thursday, May 15, 1902, when Ora McHenry and Myrtie Conneau were married in Tucson, Arizona. *The Daily Evening News* immediately reported the event, noting that "two of the most prominent and highly esteemed residents of this city" had been married at high noon in the Grace Methodist Episcopal Church in Tucson. "The bride is one of Modesto's popular belles and her marriage to one of the most prominent financiers and land owners in the valley will cause her to receive a host of happy congratulations". Then, referring to the groom, "His genial personality and enterprising mode of action in business affairs has made him one of the foremost men of the community". The couple returned to Modesto two weeks later, having honeymooned in Southern California, San Francisco, and Alameda.

It is appropriate at this point to discuss the background of Myrtie Conneau, particularly as described during an interview by Merl McHenry, who was the only child born to Myrtie and Ora. She was the daughter of Frank Ernest Conneau, originally from France, and Annie Waters, who was born in Kilkenny, Ireland. Frank Conneau was a pioneer in the manufacture of brick and lime and was responsible for the erection of some of the earliest brick structures in Modesto, including the Tynan Hotel and the Wood & Turner building on I Street. When he died in 1886, leaving six children and little money, Myrtie was just eight years old. The widowed Annie Waters Conneau spent the next years supporting her family by taking in washing and boarders. As the children grew to adulthood, she decided that she could only send two of them to college, Myrtie and William (called Albert). The family left the Conneau home on the corner of McHenry and Downey Avenue and moved to Palo Alto, where Annie continued to take in washing and boarders until Myrtie and Albert had graduated from Stanford University. The other four Conneau children were Matilda (called Tillie), Lena, Letitia (Letty), and Arthur Ernest (Ernie). Matilda, later married to George Schafer, had the distinction of being the first baby girl born in the new settlement of Modesto in 1872. Merl McHenry stated that his father, Ora, first noticed Myrtie when she was playing outside the Conneau home wearing a dress made from Sperry flour sacks. Another interesting aspect of the Conneau story, particularly in regard to the McHenry Mansion, is that the widowed mother of Annie Waters Conneau was remarried to Samuel Catts of Stockton in 1859, and they had two children named George and Margaret Catts. Margaret Catts later married Richard Lauxen. Richard and his brother-in-law, George, started a furniture store in Stockton in 1887 called Lauxen and Catts. Renowned for the fine quality of its merchandise, the store eventually occupied a five story building at the corner of San Joaquin and Weber Streets until 1934. The significance of this story to our study of the McHenry Mansion is that furnishings acquired for the house from 1902 until 1919 may well have come from the Lauxen and Catts store in Stockton. Merl McHenry remembered spending a great deal of time with Lauxen and Catts cousins as he was growing up.

The June 1902 list of school promotions included the names of Albert and Robert McHenry, promoted to the 5th and 7th grades respectively at the 14th Street School. So, the summer of 1902 found the McHenry Mansion occupied by the newlyweds and the two McHenry sons. The house was still far removed from downtown businesses in the early 1900s, although there now was a neighbor next door. Rancher John J. McMahon had married Eva May Enslen in December of 1899 and had built a large home for his bride on lots #13 through #16 (of block #122) at 16th and I Streets, across the alley from the McHenry house. The McMahons moved into their home in 1900 and played important roles in the McHenrys' lives, both socially and in business.

On Friday, July 11, 1902, Myrtie, Bob and Albert McHenry left in a camping wagon with M.L. Toomes and his wife and Mrs. L. Atkins of San Francisco, for a five week stay in Yosemite Valley and at Kennedy Lake in Tuolumne County. Two weeks later, Ora joined the party for the Yosemite portion of the vacation. Camping wagons were usually drawn by at least two horses or mules, and a cook often accompanied a party of campers. The following month, Myrtie McHenry and the two boys stayed in San Francisco.

In September 1902, Ora and Myrtie departed for a month's trip to New York and Pennsylvania, in part for the purpose of his settling a law suit that had been pending in the Philadelphia courts for two years. The suit had to do with the rights of shippers in routing goods to the eastern markets, and the jury's verdict was favorable to Ora McHenry.

The McHenry Mansion's heyday of social entertaining occurred between 1903 and mid-1905. The parties produced by Myrtie Conneau McHenry, undoubtedly with the help of her capable sisters, were certainly among the most innovative and creative in Modesto's early history. An example was the large New Year's Day party given at the house in 1903, with Myrtie's sister, Letty Conneau, serving as hostess. About 90 persons attended the afternoon affair, which was enthusiastically reported on the front page of the *Daily Evening News* and described as "the most elaborate society event of the season". The theme of the party was "hearts" with "strings of hearts, candy hearts, hearts everywhere. The home was elaborately decorated in cut flowers and smilax and every niche was filled with a heart". As the guests entered, a small bag containing a number of candy hearts was hung around his or her neck. The hearts were used for playing a conversational game in which, if a person said the words "yes" or "no" in reply to a question, he had to give the questioner a heart. Frank Cressey, Jr. got the most hearts "by his skillful talks to his friends" and won the prize, which was a silver key ring and chain. This is especially interesting, because, in 1906, Mr. Cressey married Letty Conneau at a wedding ceremony performed in the Mansion. Another game played at this party involved throwing bean bags at heart-shaped target boards located in each room. Prizes for the winners were a gold heart-shaped locket for the woman and a silver heart-shaped key ring for the man. A third game defies the imagination and can best be described by directly quoting from the newspaper article.

The next amusement was a string chewing contest. Each one present was supplied with a string at one end of which a candy heart was attached. The idea was to let the heart dangle in mid-air while the other end of the string was placed in the mouth, and then get the heart to the mouth without using one's hands.

The winner received a gold heart stick pin. Finally, all of the guests were given paper and pencil and asked to draw a likeness of someone present, which "caused great amusement. Some of the pictures were good resemblances, others, however, were pictures no artist would paint". These artistic endeavors were then pinned to the wall, and the guests were asked to guess their identities. The prize was a burnt wood toilet box. Cook's orchestra was present and "at frequent intervals during the afternoon strains of music floated through the rooms". There were also musical selections by several soloists and a recitation. Delicious refreshments were served in the elaborately decorated dining room, from a table "gorgeous in flowers and dainties", and the party broke up about 5:30.

Two days later, on a Saturday evening from 8:00 to 10:00 o'clock, the McHenrys held a reception for about 65 persons to meet an evangelist, Dr. Arthur J. Smith, and his associate, baritone singer Harper G. Smyth. The two were in Modesto to conduct what turned out to be a very successful three week "Union Revival Meeting" held at several local churches. The evening was spent "in conversation" with a number of good story tellers present, vying with each other "in a flow of wit which was highly entertaining to their auditors". Mr. Smyth

This photo of the McHenry Mansion shows the McMahon house through the trees. Note the unpaved I Street.

sang musical selections, accompanied by J.M. Howell at the piano who also played several solos. According to the *Daily News*, "The home was still radiant in its decorations of New Year's Day, and the guests were made to feel at their ease by the hospitable host and hostess. The evening's pleasure was rounded out by the singing of a parting hymn by all the guests, and a prayer by Dr. Smith".

A sidelight to the Union Revival Meeting has to do with the Front Street saloons. Esther Tennent, in her book *California Was Built*, wrote, "To the women of Modesto, Front Street did not exist. If compelled by circumstances to ride down this broad way in the protection of their men, their eyes stared straight ahead". Thus it is almost surprising that, in January of 1903, a committee of ladies went to the saloon keepers and appealed to them to close during the hours of the daily Union Revival services. The committee met with "nothing but kindness from the proprietors of those places", said the *Daily News*, and many saloon keepers agreed to close during the stated hours. The item continued, "It looks as if Modesto is certainly, at last, to have a religious awakening".

The next social event occurring at the McHenry Mansion in 1903 was on Valentines Day when, according to the *Stanislaus Weekly News*,

> The beautiful home of Mr. and Mrs. O. McHenry on Saturday afternoon presented a whirling medley of smiling faces, handsome gowns, feminine gossip and wit, the occasion being a valentine card party with which Mrs. McHenry entertained about seventy-five of her lady friends.

Again, hearts were used as the theme, with strings of red hearts suspended from the chandeliers to the corners of the rooms, with hearts dominating the tally cards, place cards, the prizes, and event the game itself (Five-handed Hearts). Ivy and smilax (a plant) were also entwined about the doorways of the home. Standing in the receiving line with Mrs. McHenry were her sister, Letty Conneau of Alameda, and the Mesdames G.P. Schafer (Matilda, another sister), J.J. McMahon (the next door neighbor), and L.W. Fulkerth (wife of the local judge). Comic valentines were given to all of the ladies, creating much amusement, and strains of music filled the house, provided by a six piece orchestra. When the game of Hearts was finished, and the scores were tallied, prizes were awarded consisting of a handpainted China jewel box in the shape of a heart (first prize), a cut glass heart shaped bon-bon dish (second), and a consolation award of a miniature pack of cards fastened to a large card on which was lettered "practice makes perfect". Finally, a "most delicious" lunch was served from the beautifully decorated table in the dining room.

Just three weeks later, on March 3, a fund-raising "Oriental Tea" was given in the Ora McHenry home in both the afternoon and evening, with a free will offering to benefit the "ladies' missionary work". A news item reported that a great deal of time and considerable money had been expended on the elaborate decorations, which were so realistic that "in fact, if a heathen Chinese were to venture in unasked he would immediately take it for a joss house and go through a number of Oriental ceremonies". Six "genuine Chinese maidens" were present to sing native songs and give short speeches wearing their native costumes, as well as a number of "counterfeit" Chinese represented by Modesto girls. Rice was served in one of the rooms, and the guests seated themselves "tailor fashion" while eating with chop sticks. Cakes and tea were also on the menu. A number of school children attended in the afternoon, and a large group of adults, including gentlemen, was present at the 6 to 9 p.m. evening tea. The ladies reportedly netted a "neat little sum" from the event.

Meanwhile, early in 1903, ten cases of small pox were reported in Modesto resulting in the quarantine of four houses. County property was going for about $35 to $50 an acre, with other prices remaining about the same. Latz's department store advertised "gents' fedora hats" at $1.95, ladies' shoes for $1.75, sleeveless vests for 10 cents per vest, Kayser fabric and silk gloves at 50 cents to $1.25, and white suede kid gloves for $1.50 a pair. Ladies' suits were $7.35 to $15 each at Meyers new store on 10th Street, and Schafer's was selling men's neckwear at two for 35 cents. Men's suits were $12 to $16, Kuppenheimer overcoats $12.50, men's outing nightshirts 58 cents and drawers 39 cents, women's French kid shoes with patent leather tips $2.50, women's stockings 25 cents a pair, ribbon girdles in pink, white, and blue for 50 cents, and rust-proof corsets were especially featured. Carpets were also being publicized at from 30 to 75 cents a yard. But perhaps the greatest excitement in Modesto during the spring of 1903 was caused by the brief visit of President Teddy Roosevelt, who gave a short speech from the back of his train at 9:30 p.m. on Monday, May 19. He was returning from Yosemite, where he had camped out with naturalist John Muir at Glacier Point and at Mariposa Big Trees. "I have seen the wonders of Yosemite," he said, "I have traveled the whole length of your beautiful San Joaquin Valley, and I am proud of the fact that such things of beauty can be found in our country".

It was announced in May of 1903 that ice manufacturing machinery had just been installed at the Bald Eagle Ranch, with a capacity of about 500 pounds of ice per day. Its purpose was to provide ice for the recently constructed modern cold storage plant, as well as for the use of the ranch employees. A large building was also being erected to house and feed the workers, which would make the ranch a model for the housing of ranch employees. Ora Louise McHenry Condrey, Ora's granddaughter who was born at the ranch and spent her early childhood there, described this building during an interview. It was like a hotel, with about 100 rooms upstairs and a large deck surrounding the building. Parties and dances were sometimes held downstairs, which had hardwood floors and was completely open. The building housed employees from other ranches, as well as those from the Bald Eagle, who came during the harvest.

Only five automobiles were owned by Modestans in 1903, according to the *Modesto Morning Herald,* and one of them belonged to Ora McHenry. An incident occurring on May 9 testifies to this fact. It was reported that Ora McHenry received a severe cut over his right eye while starting his automobile in front of his house. He was standing at the side of the car, turning the crank to start the engine, when apparently too much gasoline pumped out and in some way caused the vehicle to leap forward, throwing Mr. McHenry up against a corner. Dr. C.W. Evans took two stitches in the wound. It was also about this time that Ruth Hewitt Herbert, niece of Matilda McHenry, was visited in Farmington by Ora in his automobile. During interviews, she recalled that he took her and her brothers for a ride which greatly impressed her, because it was the first time she had ever ridden in a car. Lena Schafer Jaggard, Myrtie's niece, also stated in an interview that Ora McHenry had one of the first "steamers" (steam-powered cars) in Modesto.

The Ora McHenrys celebrated their first "paper" wedding anniversary by giving a spectacular party for two hundred guests at the Bald Eagle Ranch. Invitations to a "Bal Papiere" were mailed in advance, and the *Modesto Daily News* of May 16, 1903 described the affair, with bold headlines, on its front page. It was held in the large new building being constructed for the Bald Eagle employees, which afforded ample floor space for the dancers. The room was decorated with strips of crepe paper of "every conceivable color" festooned from the roof to the walls and with many electric light globes inside Chinese lanterns. A twelve-piece orchestra, placed on a raised platform, furnished the music. But certainly the outstanding feature of this party was that the ladies wore paper dresses.

> The scene of unusual beauty made by the bright and handsome costumes may better be imagined than described. Suffice it to say that every gown in the room was handsome, and displayed taste and art upon the part of the makers. There were paper dresses of every hue, many of them decorated with roses and other flowers, which heightened the charming effect of the whole room. When the dancing started the floor was a maze of color and grace.

Each lady brought a paper necktie that matched her gown, and these were collected and distributed among the gentlemen at the beginning of the party. The men then found their partners for the grand march by matching their ties with the ladies' gowns. "The grand march was led by about a dozen handsomely arrayed young ladies and gentlemen, and all of the dancers participated". The waltz and two-step were among the dances featured. At midnight, the guests adjourned to the second floor, where long tables had been set up with refreshments. Dancing was then resumed until after 1 o'clock. The news item commented that Mrs. McHenry had been ill for some time prior to the party but was able to enjoy the "manifest pleasure" of the others. According to family members, a French seamstress, who often stayed at the McHenry home for as long as two weeks to "outfit" the family, produced Myrtie's and her sisters' paper dresses for this special party.

Later that year, on December 3, 1903, Myrtie and Ora's son, Merl, was born in the McHenry Mansion, in the bedroom adjoining the upstairs sitting room according to Merl. He referred to it as the "blue room" because of the color of the wall paper and curtains.

1904 was an eventful year both for Modesto and the Ora McHenry family. The city's Jubilee celebration in April, honoring the completion of the Modesto-Turlock irrigation system, was a great success and a personal triumph for ardent irrigationist Ora McHenry. It was also a time of considerable expansion for the McHenry business enterprises, including the First National Bank. At the bank's annual meeting in January, a change of officers occurred, with the election of Ora McHenry, president; Garrison Turner, vice president; J.E. Ward, cashier; and G.R. Stoddard, assistant cashier. Then, by January 15, all but the "finishing touches" had been put on the bank's new building, and its tenants were settled in their "bright new offices and rooms" and open for business. Located on the northwest corner of 10th and I Streets, the building was described as "a very handsome affair and one of which Modesto people may show to the newcomers here with no small amount of pride". Tenants included Moss Rose Confectionary on the ground floor and, in the upstairs portion, two dentists and a tailor. Those final finishing touches apparently required another seven months, because the bank itself did not open its doors until August 13, 1904, when a news item proclaimed "There is no bank in the entire San Joaquin Valley to equal the new home of the First National Bank at 10th and I Streets".

Portrait of Albert McHenry.

Modesto was making great progress by 1904, mostly due to the arrival of irrigation, and had a growing population of 2500, up from 2040 in 1900. It was announced that the Sunset Telegraph and Telephone Company was raising its rates from $1.00 to $1.25 per month for service on a ten party line. By now, Modesto had 16 ten party lines to residences and 10 ten party lines to businesses, and the McHenrys were among those with telephones. A major topic under discussion in the community concerned the desirability of numbering the houses. In June 1904, the Modesto Board of Trustees resolved the problem by hiring the Weber Number Manufacturing Company for the purpose of numbering businesses and houses within the city. The task was to be completed by August 1, 1904 at a charge no greater than 40 cents per house. Thus, the McHenry Mansion acquired its street number of 906 (15th Street) in the summer of 1904. It was also about this time that Modesto barbers agreed on a new fee schedule: haircuts, 35 cents; shampoo, 25 cents; whiskers trimmed, any style, 25 cents; and moustaches curled, 10 cents.

McHenry parties at the Mansion continued to make news, including one headlined "Young Folks Had A Delightful Time" recounted in the *Stanislaus County News* of February 5, 1904. Hosts were Bob and Albert McHenry, and the evening's entertainment was an "exciting" new game called *Pit,* "a most mirth-provoking game, and the players shouted and screamed with laughter". Piano selections and a piccolo solo followed, after which the 24 guests were ushered from the parlor to the dining room where "was spread a sumptuous repast". Then, it was back to the parlor for more piano playing until after midnight.

Another of Modesto's famous leap year balls was held on February 29, 1904 with Mrs. Ora McHenry serving on the planning committee of nine members. Pronounced a "grand success", the dance was held in Armory Hall which was elaborately decorated in red and green under the guidance of "an expert from San Francisco". Many of the ladies' gowns were described in the *Stanislaus Weekly News,* with Mrs. McHenry listed as wearing "blue crepe de chine over blue silk". Following the dance, the ladies of the committee and their escorts adjourned to the McHenry home, where an elegant dinner was served. "The hospitable home was charmingly decorated for the occasion and the viands which were served were greatly enjoyed by the guests", said the *News.* This story takes on special significance when it is recalled that Ora McHenry attended Modesto's first leap year ball, held at Rogers Hall in 1880 (see page 39).

One of Modesto's most historic events occurred on April 22 and 23 of 1904, and Ora McHenry was a member of the general planning committee. Called the Irrigation Jubilee, the joyful celebration marked the end of the area's nearly 20 year struggle for irrigation and, as described in the *San Francisco Chronicle,* "the completion of the system which brings under irrigation 260,000 acres of as good land as lies outdoors". Jointly sponsored by citizens of both Modesto and Turlock, 30 railroad cars brought many of the 5000 visitors to the little town of 2500 population, including California Governor and Mrs. George Pardee and University of California President Benjamin Ide Wheeler. The throng of citizens and visitors cheered as Modesto's street lights were all turned on at the same time. Events included formal ceremonies in Courthouse Park, parades, fireworks, music by bands and choruses, lunch served outdoors in a vacant lot at the corner of 11th and I Streets, train tours of the irrigated lands throughout the county, guided tours of the La Grange Dam, and grand balls at the Armory and Plato Halls.

Hearts was the featured game at the Ora McHenrys' second wedding anniversary party, given at their home on May 16, 1904. About 30 friends attended the informal affair, which featured music as well as the card games, with refreshments served late in the evening.

Summer of 1904 found many Modestans again leaving the hot weather for the coast. Bob and Albert McHenry departed on July 15 for a summer stay at Santa Cruz, and their parents spent some time in San Francisco. In August, the Brooklyn Hotel on Front Street was destroyed by fire, and Ora McHenry, who owned the building in which the hotel was located, was interviewed at the site. He stated that he would replace the structure with a three story brick hotel, for which he already had the plans. It was also noted that he held insurance on the building, with a company for which he was the Modesto agent.

On September 8, 1904, Ora and Myrtie McHenry and her sister, Letty Conneau, left for San Francisco by train, enroute to New York via Vancouver on the Canadian Pacific Railroad. They also visited Cleveland and the St. Louis World's Fair. While they were gone, San Francisco and Modesto newspapers carried extensive articles telling of the incorporation of the O. McHenry Packing Company, formed with a capital of one million dollars. It was announced that Ora McHenry was building a $500,000 packing and slaughtering plant at the Bald Eagle Ranch and a large refrigeration plant in Oakland, where a valuable wharf site had already been purchased. Of the total amount, Ora McHenry subscribed $940,000, and six friends and associates invested $10,000 each: attorney L.L. Dennett, J.E. Ward, G.P. Schafer, G.R. Stoddard, John Dunn, Jr. and Ernest Conneau. All but Dennett were connected with the McHenry banking, farming, or merchandising interests. An October 6, 1904 article in the *San Francisco Chronicle* stated that this would be the largest concern of its kind in the West, noting that the 4000 acre Bald Eagle was probably the best equipped ranch in the state and would be included in the Corporation. Also planned was an electric railroad running from Modesto to the ranch. It was revealed that one of the purposes of Mr. McHenry's trip East was to make a study of the big packing plants and stock yards of the Eastern cities.

1905 began auspiciously at the Mansion, with a New Year's Eve party hosted by the McHenrys for 30 invited guests. As usual, the *Stanislaus County News* exuded enthusiasm: "The spacious rooms had been artistically decorated for the occasion, and canvas stretched for dancing, which amusement the guests indulged in, the laws of leap year being adhered to". A "dainty" supper was served following the dancing. Then, in February, the Ora McHenrys gave another party at their home for thirty "young folks", in honor of their guest, Miss Lita Lauxen of Stockton. Again, according to the *Stanislaus News* of February 17, 1904, "canvas was spread over the carpets of three of the large rooms, and with Cook's orchestra of three pieces stationed in the hall, the conditions for dancing were ideal". The waltz and two step dances were enjoyed by the "merry throng of dancers", with punch available in the dining room between dances and other "delicious refreshments" served later.

The memories of two long-time area residents have given us firsthand descriptions of McHenry teenage parties that occurred in the time frame of 1902-05. Goldie Davis, who was a teenager during this era, attended a party at the Mansion with Ora's oldest son, Bob McHenry, as her escort. This, in fact, was her first date. During interviews, she described being called for by young Bob in a horse and buggy and traveling up the unpaved I Street to the McHenry home, where a groom came out and took the buggy. She recalled the canvas stretched over the carpets in the big rooms for dancing and an orchestra playing in the "office at the left of the front door". She remembered placing her coat upstairs, in a bedroom at the top of the stairway where a fire was burning in a fireplace and where Mrs. McHenry was sitting on a chaise lounge greeting guests. Another visitor to the house at this time was Ruth Hewitt Herbert, niece of Matilda McHenry and second cousin of Ora, who recalled traveling by train from Stockton with her mother and staying overnight at the McHenrys. A party was being given for Bob and Albert, and she watched the dancers from the stairway, also observing the canvas stretched over the carpets.

One of the most elaborate parties given by the McHenrys was a St.

Patrick's Day costume dance given on Friday night, March 17, 1905. Attended by a total of 70 persons, 40 costumed and 30 not in costume, the party was "the most unique, gorgeous and delightful affairs in the annals of social events in Modesto for many a day" according to the *Stanislaus News*. Important to our study of the McHenry Mansion is the house's description as the setting for the party.

> The McHenry home must have been designed for just such functions as that within its walls last evening. The rooms are spacious and admit of the most charming decorations, which last night were exceedingly appropriate, conforming in idea with the day which the affair was designed to celebrate. The carpets of the large rooms and halls were covered with canvas.

The party decorations were described in detail, as was also the menu of the supper served at 1 a.m. and the costumes worn by some of the guests, including Ora and Myrtie McHenry who were dressed as an Indian chief and Indian maiden. The story of this party is reprinted in its entirety in Appendix D.

Ora and Myrtie McHenry celebrated their third wedding anniversary by inviting 50 friends to an 8 p.m. card party, at which the game of the evening was Progressive Euchre. The rooms were decorated in red, using large bunches of scarlet carnations, red rambler roses and red poppies, with smilax entwining the chandeliers. Refreshments were served at the card tables during the evening.

Many of the early-day parties given at the Mansion followed a similar pattern: a large number of guests entertained in the downstairs double parlors and library, with food served from the table in the dining room; a specific party theme carefully carried out in decorations, favors, and prizes; elaborate decorations often hanging from the chandeliers, in the open doorways, and on the dining table; music provided by a small orchestra usually stationed in the entrance hall and perhaps occasionally in the office; frequently a soloist singing to piano accompaniment, with further piano solos by the accompanist; sometimes, recitations as well as music; and games played by the guests, either informally and of a humorous nature and/or formal card games such as Hearts or Euchre. When dancing was on the agenda, the furniture was removed and the carpets were covered with canvas, waxed to make it slick, stretched taut and attached to hooks around the floorboards.

Ora McHnery's business activities were still growing in the first half of 1905. In January, the First National Bank of Modesto purchased two lots in Turlock and began construction of that city's first bank. Called the First National Bank of Turlock, it opened for business in July, and Ora was the largest stockholder and president. At the same time, the Modesto Bank was also expanding and, in March, filed Articles of Incorporation for the formation of the Modesto Savings Bank, with Ora McHenry as the majority stock shareholder. It was announced that the officers would be the same as for the Modesto Bank. Also in March, Ora purchased the Fresno Meat Company for $30,000 enabling the McHenry Meat Packing Company to supply meat to markets in Fresno and vicinity. "It is probable that Modesto will become the supply center for a large number of butcher shops in many towns of California, thanks to the enterprise of Mr. McHenry", said the *Stanislaus News*.

In September 1905, Modesto newspapers featured articles reconfirming the sound financial condition of the First National Bank, relevant to a run on the bank by nervous depositors that had recently occurred. The cause of public anxiety about the bank was attributd to the recent failure of the Bank of Oakdale and the rumored ill health of Ora McHenry. A telegram received from the First National Bank of San Francisco reassured investors, stating "If required, your bank can have all the money needed to settle with all depositors in full". An item in the *Stanislaus Weekly News* of September 22 reported that lack of confidence in the bank had been completely unfounded, noting,

> O. McHenry is a capitalist and a progressive one. He is a money maker and a money handler of rare ability. He has done more in a financial way and in the way of Stanislaus development than any other man in the county and is ready to continue the good work. There is absolutely no good reason why the people should not have confidence in him and his business associates.

In November, a state bank examiner issued a statement, following his examination of the First National and Union Savings Banks, declaring both to be "in the best of shape". Unfortunately, by this time Ora McHenry was not in as good a shape as his banks and had health problems that seemed to be worsening.

THE FINAL MONTHS, 1905-1906

Ora and Myrtie McHenry returned from a stay at Adams Springs in September 1905, where it was hoped that the waters would help the stomach ailment that had been troubling him. However, his condition did not improve, and on Thursday, September 28, he was operated on at Adler's Sanitarium in San Francisco for "a malignant growth upon his intestines". The operation was pronounced a success, and he returned to Modesto on October 27 to convalesce at his home. Two weeks later the *Stanislaus Weekly News* reported that "O. McHenry was out driving Tuesday and appears much better than he has been for weeks. He is now able to come down stairs without assistance which is remarkable considering that his severe illness is only a thing of the very recent past". Later that month, he drove his car downtown and was seen at the bank.

Meanwhile, young Bob McHenry, by now 18 years old, was enrolled at Santa Clara College and made the headlines in the *Stanislaus News* of December 15, 1905, as "The Poet of Santa Clara". His poem on school life "will appeal to all *News* readers who have ever attended boarding school" said the article, which also printed the poem.

Only twelve more days for me
In this place of misery.
No more Latin, no more Greek,
No more smoking on the sneak.
No more sand fleas in my tea,
Making goo-goo eyes at me.
No more bed-bugs in my bed,
"No more mush", the waiter said.
No more study -- recreation,
Everything is recreation.

Ah! At last I am now free,
From the stew and soda tea;
From the white-washed highboard fence,
From prefects, knocking, complements,
From sticky, rotten mud and slush;
From hash and spuds and burning mush;
From eggs from which the chickens peep,
From beds in which I cannot sleep;
From waiters who bring grub too slow,
I'll leave them all for Mo-des-to.

Now that I'm at home, sweet home,
I doubt if back again I'll roam,
To that crazy, bughouse school,
Where all is taught by rote or rule;
Never more that voice I'll hear,
That in the morning sounds so clear;
But alas! It's this I fear --
I'll go back again next year.

On January 11, 1906, Oramil and Myrtie Conneau McHenry were reunited in marriage by Judge L.W. Fulkerth, presumably at the McHenry Mansion. The purpose, according to the *Daily Evening News*, was to avoid any future problems in regard to property rights that might arise from the fact that their original marriage had been solemnized in Arizona before his California divorce had been finalized. Although at that time California recognized the legality of out-of-state marriages, this was undoubtely part of Ora's efforts to get his affairs in order during his final illness. It was later revealed that, during the last months before his death, he sold his interest in the Modesto Bank and transferred to his wife, Myrtie, various assets including his controlling stock in the G.P. Schafer Company, 4000 acres of land not included in the Bald Eagle Ranch, and all of his stock in Modesto's First National and Union Savings Banks and the First National Bank of Turlock, thereby giving her control of these institutions. His will, described below, was signed just two weeks before the remarriage ceremony, on December 27.

Oramil McHenry died at his home on Wednesday afternoon, February 21, 1906 at age 44 "in the midst of his usefulness", to quote an obituary. The *Stanislaus Weekly News* described him as "owning more wealth than any man in Stanislaus County" and as "one of the enterprising and prominent figures of Central California, devoting his money to many commercial affairs in this vicinity and thereby doing much to develop the new West". It elaborated on his many contributions to the irrigation movement, stating

In the passing of Ora McHenry, Modesto loses a man who was always foremost in the work of her advancement; Stanislaus County one who did more toward her development than any other power, and California one of her prominent, substantial, enterprising capitalists, such a one as she can ill afford to lose.

His memberships in local organizations were listed, including the First Presbyterian Church, Stanislaus Masonic Lodge #206, Stockton Lodge #218 B.P.O.E., and the Native Sons of the Golden West. His body lay in state in the McHenry home from 10 until 4:00 o'clock on February 23, and the funeral was held the following day, on Saturday at 10 a.m. Modesto businesses and banks closed during the services, and many flags in the city were flown at half-mast. The long funeral procession made its way from the McHenry home to the Masonic Cemetery, where Ora McHenry was buried in the family plot. A newspaper account of the funeral appears in Appendix E.

...OFFICES OF...
THE FIRST NATIONAL BANK
...AND...
UNION SAVINGS BANK

Modesto, Cal.,
Feb. 25, 1906

Dear Sir:
It is with deep sorrow that we announce the death of Mr. O. McHenry, President of these Banks, at his home in Modesto, Cal., Feb. 21, 1906.
Yours respectfully,
J.E. Ward,
Cashier

The March 2, 1906 issue of the *Stanislaus Weekly News* had many columns devoted to the McHenrys. An outline of Ora's financial assets was given on page one, and a copy of his will, in its entirety, took up about half of page three. Also in this issue was the announcement that Mrs. Myrtie McHenry had been selected as president of the First National and Union Savings Banks by the Board of Directors and would replace her husband as a director of both banks. The will was filed for probate by custodian John J. McMahon, who was the McHenrys' neighbor and friend. The total value of the estate was listed at $1,062,060 and included large holdings in the O. McHenry Company, the Stanislaus Development Company, the First National Bank of San Francisco, The Grange Company, and the Herald Publishing Company, as well as $22,500 in Modesto Irrigation District bonds, life insurance policies totaling $109,335, interest in a Salida warehouse, and considerable property in and around Modesto and other areas such as in Oakland, Fresno, and Kern County. Myrtie McHenry was interviewed by a reporter following her appointment as president of the banks and made assurances that she had no intention of selling the bank stock, that "the solid assets of the various financial institutions in which my late husband was interested will continue just the same", and that she was worth approximately $600,000 which "will be used as Mr. McHenry himself would have used it". This obviously was to reassure depositors and prevent any possible run on the banks as had happened previously. Although her stock in the First National Bank of Turlock was sold in November 1906, Myrtie McHenry remained president of the First National and Union Savings Banks until 1910.

Under the terms of Ora McHenry's will, his wife received the house and property at 15th and I Streets, as well as 4750 of the total 10,000 shares of the capital stock of the O. McHenry Company, which included the 4000 acre Bald Eagle Ranch. The three sons, Bob, Albert, and Merl each were given 1750 shares of O. McHenry stock, and all other properties and possessions were to be shared equally by the family members. Former brother-in-law Albert C. Bilicke was named as financial guardian for sons Bob and Albert, to manage and invest their portions of the estate until they reached age 28. Bilicke had become very successful in Southern California real estate investing, as well as in hotel management.

Ora McHenry's influence on Modesto was felt long after his death, in part because of his donation of a library to the city. Under the terms of his will, property comprising three lots and the sum of $20,000 were bequeathed to the city of Modesto for the purpose of erecting and establishing a public library building. The will also stipulated that the first Board of Trustees be composed of Myrtie McHenry, L.W. Fulkerth, John Ross, J.J. McMahon, and L.L. Dennett. See Chapter 6 for further discussion of this bequest.

THE END OF AN ERA

The passing of Oramil McHenry marked the end of the most significant era in the history of the McHenry Mansion. This period, dating from the beginning of the home's construction in 1882 until Ora's death in 1906, represented the founding and growth of a town, as well as the story of a house and the people who lived in it. The numerous contributions of Robert and Ora McHenry, father and son, to the development and prosperity of Modesto and the rich central valley of

California were immense. An article published in the *Modesto Morning Herald* on November 11, 1911 eloquently summed up the McHenry legacy. Penned by an anonymous writer of the day who called himself "The Old Timer", it said, in part, "Of the men who made their influence felt in the development and upbuilding of Stanislaus County, none accomplished more than did the late Robert McHenry and his son, Oramil". Continuing, the article described Robert as a man of great business ability by which he amassed a fortune, but while "gaining wealth for himself he was ever ready to lend a helping hand to his neighbors who were less fortunate and to aid public enterprises by his counsel and money, thus proving himself a benefactor in every worthy cause". Ora received even more praise, for his development of the "model" McHenry ranch with its "extensive orchards, the flourishing alfalfa fields, the many attractive farm buildings including meat markets, shops, box factories, drying houses and other buildings" as well as his supervision of meat markets throughout the San Joaquin Valley with headquarters in Oakland, and his presidency of the First National Bank. "But those were not his greatest achievements", said the writer.

> By his superior business tact and universal popularity as a business man, he was instrumental in bringing prosperity and contentment to hundreds of homes by distributing water on nearly 100,000 acres of fertile land, a large portion of which now blooms like a rose. To accomplish this great project, aided by a few heroic business men of the Modesto irrigation district who could see the incalculable benefits to be derived from irrigation, Mr. McHenry spent money with a lavish hand and talked irrigation to men of influence. The great work was finally put through and he proved himself a masterful leader in a great enterprise.

Now this story of the McHenry Mansion moves on to a new phase and changing times.

Widow Myrtie McHenry and son, Merl.

CHAPTER 5

A QUIET TIME

Myrtie Conneau McHenry was just 27 years old when she was widowed in February 1906. She was left with great wealth, business responsibilities, and a two year old son, Merl. Stepsons Bob and Albert McHenry were away at school, and it was a quiet time at the McHenry Mansion. Myrtie's mother, Annie Waters Conneau, probably lived in the house during this period, in the front bedroom to the right of the stairs on the second floor, according to Merl McHenry. Merl's bedroom was above the dining room, at the rear of the house facing I Street, and he stated that his Aunt Lena Conneau, sister of Myrtie, occupied the Blue Room next to the sitting room for "a long time".

The great San Francisco earthquake of April 18, 1906 was the subject of a news story featuring Robert and Albert McHenry who, on that date, returned to Modesto from Santa Clara and reported that both San Jose and Santa Clara were in ruins. Santa Clara College and the business houses in the town were practically destroyed, they said. Later that month, the *Stanislaus Weekly News* reported, "Mrs. McHenry is entertaining as guests Mrs. Hewitt and children from Stockton". One of those children was Ruth Herbert who, during an interview, recalled making the train trip from Stockton with her mother and brothers to pay their respects to Mrs. McHenry. They stayed overnight, and she remembered that they all sat in the upstairs sitting room and talked. Her special memory was of climbing up a staircase into the cupola, which at that time had a floor, with baby Merl going along with a nurse or maid. The third floor was an attic used for storage, she said.

The McHenry Mansion was the setting for a June wedding in 1906 when Letty Conneau, sister of Myrtie, was married to Frank Cressey, Jr., at such an early hour that the June 8 newspaper headline read, "Young People United and Leave on Honeymoon While Town Slumbers". With only the families present, the ceremony was "characterized by extreme simplicity, but few flowers being used, and the wedding service being brief". The bride wore a Panama traveling suit, and after the ceremony the happy newlyweds "entered an automobile" and, accompanied by a party of relatives, were driven to Salida where they took the northbound train. A number of friends had boarded the train at Modesto and "overhauled the pair at Salida, giving them laughing congratulations". The honeymoon was spent in San Jose and Pacific Grove, after which the couple lived in a "cottage on 15th Street". Unfortunately, this marriage ended in divorce in 1913.

During the summer months of 1906, Myrtie spent time with her family, the Conneaus, at Pacific Grove, and San Francisco and San Jose were also travel destinations. Meanwhile, the Women's Improvement Club, organized in April 1906 to improve and beautify Modesto, was recommending that the streets be paved. And a petition was being circulated and "heavily signed" concerning bicycle riding in the town. It proposed that

any person riding a bicycle along any public street, sidewalk, alley, or thoroughfare within the limits of the city of Modesto must have a bell attached to each bicycle and must ring the bell loudly and continuously at least 30 feet before reaching and traversing each public street crossing.

In October, San Francisco District Attorney William Langdon spoke at a meeting of the Independence League of California, held at the Armory in Modesto. He received the League's endorsement for governor, although George Gillett was the eventual winner of the California governorship (Read on to discover how this item relates to our McHenry Mansion story). Also in a political vein, in November the McHenry neighbor, John J. McMahon, was elected to the Board of Supervisors.

In an election held on November 4, 1907, William H. Langdon, known as the "graft prosecuting" District Attorney of San Francisco, was elected to his second two year term. Four days later, local news articles reported his presence at the home of Mrs. Myrtie McHenry in Modesto, where he was relaxing from the strenuous political campaign. He was accompanied by two aides from his office, one of whom was a Conneau relative named Mark Noone. The group attended the circus in Modesto and spent time at the Bald Eagle Ranch. In just two months, headlines in the *Stanislaus Weekly News* announced that Myrtie McHenry was betrothed to District Attorney Langdon, explaining that the romance had begun when Mr. Langdon had visited the McHenry home with Mark Noone the previous summer.

Probably the last large party given in the McHenry Mansion by Myrtie McHenry before her marriage to William Langdon occurred on St. Patrick's Day, March 19, 1908. More than 75 ladies attended the event, which the *Stanislaus Weekly News* declared "an unqualified success". The "spacious rooms of the McHenry residence were beautifully decorated for the occasion", gushed the *News,* and cards constituted the afternoon's entertainment. The tallies were so arranged as to represent the Patron Saint of Ireland, and "dainty refreshments were also a reminder of the good saint of the Irish".

Now, in the spring of 1908, the McHenry Mansion was about to see a change of tenants and, ultimately, a different way of life within its walls.

Mrs. Mrytie McHenry left this morning for San Francisco to remain until after New Year's. She will be joined on Wednesday by Miss Lena Conneau and Miss Theresa Grollman, who with other friends will form a theater and dinner party that night.

MODESTO DAILY EVENING NEWS
December 30, 1907

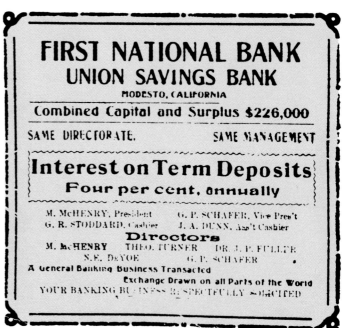

Portrait of Judge William Langdon.

CHAPTER 6

THE WORLD OF THE LANGDONS

A NEW BEGINNING 1908-1909

On April 20, 1908, a very special wedding occurred at the McHenry Mansion, uniting "the wealthiest and most popular lady in Stanislaus County", and the "instigator of graft prosecution of San Francisco". The *Stanislaus Weekly News* declared,

> Probably no wedding that has ever taken place in California has created a greater furor than did the wedding today of Mrs. Myrtie McHenry, owner of the Bald Eagle Ranch and President of the First National Bank of Modesto, and Mr. William H. Langdon, District Attorney of San Francisco. The eyes of the whole country were turned toward Modesto when it became rumored abroad that District Attorney Langdon had stolen away from hurly burly and bustle in bringing high offenders to justice for the purpose of coming to 'Sunny Stanislaus', where he had wooed and won a bride. The telephone lines into Modesto were sizzling this afternoon with eager inquiries from the leading dailies of the country, anxious for news of the wedding.

Only a few family members were in attendance when the couple stood before an altar "profusely banked" with flowers for the simple ceremony. The service was read by the Reverend Father Otis of San Francisco, who was a close personal friend of the groom's. The *News* reported that "the bride never looked sweeter than today, when she was led to the altar by the stalwart leader of the San Francisco graft prosecution". So quiet and simple was the late morning ceremony, however, that no one knew about it until it was over and the pair had been whisked away to Turlock, where they boarded the southbound noon train. An amusing aside to this event was the fact that the bride and groom refused to give their ages to the county clerk when applying for a marriage license, stating merely that they were "over 18" and "over 21". Their true ages were 29 and 34. The newlyweds moved into a home in San Francisco, but Myrtie McHenry-Langdon, as she was now referred to in the newspapers, was soon making trips back to Modesto.

Thus began what could be called the "political phase" of the McHenry Mansion history, representing the final years that the bulding was occupied as a single family home. It was an interesting era, stretching from 1908 to 1919.

In November of 1908, an accident occurred in front of Modesto High School, which at that time was located at 12th and L Streets. Involved were William Langdon's sisters, Sally and Margaret, Lena Conneau and Merl McHenry, who happened to be passing by the school in their horse-drawn carriage while the Modesto High-Lowell High School track meet was in progress. The report of the starter's pistol frightened the horse which turned sharply and overturned the buggy, hurling all four occupants to the ground as the animal went racing down the street. The *Stanislaus News* vividly described the scene.

> Athletes rushed to the rescue, and before the young ladies had hardly touched the ground, a dozen sturdy sprinters and hurdlers were by their side and strong arms were lifting them from the dust of the roadway where they had been thrown. Meantime, other fleet runners had overtaken the runaway horse, not, however, before it had demolished the overturned buggy.

The summoned Dr. C.W. Evans declared that none of the victims had been injured, and they were moved "to the home of Mrs. Langdon" to rest. Merl McHenry was only five years old when this incident occurred, but it apparently impressed him because he described it during an interview. Incidentally, the accident was costly, because the price of a buggy varied from about $100 to $250, depending upon the size and model.

For the next year, Myrtie and William Langdon traveled back and forth between San Francisco and Modesto. By now, young Bob McHenry had graduated from Foster Preparatory School at Litchfield, Connecticut and Santa Clara College and, according to Tinkham, joined District Attorney Langdon's staff in 1908 as a special agent during the graft prosecution in San Francisco. Following the trial, Bob returned home to manage the Bald Eagle Ranch. Meanwhile, brother Albert was studying at Belmont Military Academy. It is also noteworthy that one of the deputies on the Langdon staff was Hiram Johnson, later to become Governor of California and United States Senator, who would play an important role in the life of his good friend, Bill Langdon.

About this time, Modesto was in what could be called its "paving period". The city's Trustees established a number of specifications for the paving of the dirt streets and sidewalks using asphalt macadam. Then they adopted ordinances sanctioning the paving of individual streets, one by one, usually over the objections of cost-conscious property owners who filed "protests to street paving". In March of 1909, the Board received an estimate of costs for paving and installing curbs and gutters on I Street from 12th to 17th Streets, with written protests immediately filed and denied. Then in October, another petition was presented to the Board pertaining to the paving of 15th Street. Signed by a number of the area's residents, it was called "Bertram's Petition", referring to Gustav Bertram who had built a home across from the McHenry Mansion on the opposite corner of 15th and I Streets in 1904. The petition requested that, before being paved, the 80 foot wide 15th street be narrowed to 40 feet to allow for 10 to 12 feet of automobile parking space down the center of the

The Gustav Bertram home, built in 1904, was opposite the Mansion, on the south corner of 15th and I Streets.

71

street, with 20 foot sidewalks. At the same time another petition was filed, in protest to Bertram's document (a protest to the protest!) and among those signers was "M. Langdon" who was listed as having 250 feet of property on 15th. Bertram's measure failed to pass on a split vote, and both 15th and I Streets were finally paved in 1910.

While all this was happening to the streets around the Mansion, the construction of a "City Barn" may have gone unnoticed. Built in late 1909 at a cost of $860, which included two coats of paint, the barn was located at the corner of 17th and H Streets, just three blocks from the Langdon home. Meanwhile, by the end of that year, the Langdon family was back home in Modesto where Christmas was observed, with the District Attorney arriving from San Francisco on December 23rd. The Christmas tree was probably placed in the library, which was its usual location according to Merl McHenry.

BUSY TIMES AT THE MANSION, 1910-1919

1910 was a year of change for the Langdons. In January, baby Lois Ann was born at home. And, in the same month, it was announced that former San Francisco District Attorney William H. Langdon, who had declined to run for a third term and now resided in Modesto, had been named as president and a director of the First National Bank, replacing Myrtie McHenry-Langdon. The following month, he denied rumors that he was interested in running for the California Senate, stating "Personally, I am out of the political running. I stated absolutely, when I left the District Attorney's office, that I would not again become a candidate for public office."

Thus the McHenry Mansion, which now was being referred to as the Langdon House, again became a family home, this time for the Langdons with new baby Lois, son Merl by now enrolled at the 14th Street Grammar School, and probably some of the Conneus such as Lena. Myrtie's mother, Annie Conneu, lived in the house until May of 1910 when she died, according to Merl, in her little room at the top of the front stairs. She was 63 years old and had been ill for some time. Her private funeral was held at the Langdon home on May 14, 1910, with Reverand H. K. Pitman of the Presbyterian Church officiating, and she was buried in the St. Stanislaus Catholic Cemetery in Modesto. Her remains were later moved to the Acacia (Masonic) Memorial Cemetery, probably sometime after August 1940 (see Chapter 7).

Final settlement of the Oramil McHenry estate occurred in 1910, when many of the original properties were sold. Bob and Albert McHenry filed articles of incorporation for the "McHenry Brothers Company," capitalized at $250,000, giving them full ownership of the Bald Eagle Ranch. The Company's Board of Directors was made up of familiar names in the McHenry history: A.C. Bilicke of Los Angeles (the boys' uncle and guardian), G.R. Stoddard, and J.M. Walthall. As it became known that the McHenry estate money would soon be available for the building of the new library, controversy arose concerning its location. Under the terms of the will, three lots on 10th

McHenry Library, Modesto, California.

The new McHenry Library, donated by Ora McHenry, was dedicated in 1912. It was on the corner of 14th and I Streets.

Street near H had been donated for the library, plus $20,000 for construction costs. Since Modesto now had a population of 4034, with downtown traffic congestion and noise, many felt that 10th Street was no longer an appropriate site. Finally, in September, a library committee purchased two lots on the corner of 14th and I Streets for $5000, directly opposite the 14th Street School, for the future library. The committee also announced plans to sell the original 10th Street lots, which eventually brought $10,000 to the project. The *Modesto Daily News* stated that Mrs. Myrtie McHenry-Langdon was "delighted with the site and believes it will find favor with the entire city." It was also noted that both I and 14th Streets were newly paved, making the library location even more desirable. Construction of the McHenry Library was begun in October 1911, under the supervision of the library committee designated in Ora McHenry's will (see Chapter 4), and was dedicated at ceremonies on April 29, 1912. Judge L.W. Fulkerth, in a speech, lauded Oramil McHenry for his generosity and also Mrs. Langdon whom, he stated, deserved a great deal of the credit "not only for the bequest in which she advised her husband but for the fine work on the completed building, as she had given a great deal of attention to the selection of plans and the carrying on of the construction and the furnishing." Merl McHenry checked out the first book from his family's library, and he said that he was most embarrassed to discover some two years later that he had failed to return it. "I must owe you a fortune in fines," he told librarian Cornelia Provines, but she said 'Considering that it was the first book, there'll be no charge."

1910 was a good year for Modesto. The street paving program was progressing, and the Women's Improvement Club was busily beautifying roads and establishing parks. A new city charter, passed in September by a vote of 432 to 72, established a commission form of government, removing partisan party politics from local government for the first time. The city purchased a greatly needed team of horses and double set of harnesses for the fire department, and more automobiles were being seen around town. Prices for big cars were high, up to $2650 for a "Speedwell 50" not including the top, and

MODESTO CITY ORDINANCE
REGULATING THE DRIVING OF
LOOSE STOCK THROUGH THE TOWN
1910

$1690 for a Maxwell four door. Smaller cars, such as the Maxwell "Runabout" or "Cup Defender," were in the $900 range. These must have seemed exorbitant when compared with prices of other kinds of goods such as meat at Kincaid & Son's, with "prompt delivery," where a porterhouse steak cost 15 cents a pound, a prime rib roast 12½ cents a pound, and a rump roast 9 cents per pound. Other prices were comparable. Schafers store advertised table salt, 50 pounds for 35 cents; None Such Mince Meat, 10 cents; rice, 20 pounds for $1.00; California bacon, 16 cents a pound; and picnic ham, 13 cents a pound. Clothing prices were not greatly different from those in 1890, with men's suits $8.50 to $15.00, women's suits $13.75, women's hosiery for 25 cents and shoes for $2.00. The Rochdale Company on 11th Street also advertised all wool Bolivian blankets at $4.48, muslin petticoats at 48 cents, and 11 cents for handkerchiefs. 400 acres of unimproved land four miles out of town were $90 an acre, with 40 acres of improved land two miles from town priced at $125 per acre but "worth $200 within a year." However, the town was not yet cosmopolitan, as evidenced by a complaint in the *Stanislaus News* that bands of loose cattle had been racing across Graceada Park, cavorting on the lawns, breaking down trees, and "trampling tender young plants and shrubbery."

1911 brought further changes in the fortunes of the Langdon-McHenry families. In January, W.H. Langdon, now president of the O. McHenry Meat Company, announced the closing of the Company's meat packing business in Fresno. Then in March, the controlling interest in the First National and Union Savings Banks was sold in "one of the biggest business deals ever made in this section of the state," according to the *Modesto Morning Herald*. The new owners were a group of "Eastern and local capitalists." William Langdon was quoted as saying that this sale would relieve him of constant attendance at the Bank, allowing him more time for his San Francisco law practice in the firm of Bartlett and Langdon. It was also revealed that the McHenry Brothers were closing out their stock-breeding interests and would be raising chickens on an extensive scale at the Bald Eagle Ranch. A year later, in August of 1912, the O. McHenry Company finally was dissolved by Judge L.W. Fulkerth, at the request of the stockholders.

About this time, the names of automobile buyers were being listed in the newspapers, and W.H. Langdon was reported to have purchased a "new Hupmobile Runabout of the torpedo type" in 1911, and a Cadillac two years later. However, cars were still scarce, and as late as 1915 there was community demand for covered hitching posts in town so that farmers could leave their teams and horses protected from bad weather.

William Langdon's association and friendship with Hiram Johnson, who was elected Governor of California in 1910, resulted in three major appointments that would shape the lives of the Langdons. Each of these involved the setting up of a newly created legislative body, reflecting the growth of Modesto and the state. The first two had to do with education, resulting from Langdon's early years in that field.

Although he had studied law in his early twenties, and was admitted to the Bar at age 23, he taught school and became the principal of schools in Fresno, San Leandro, and San Francisco. He was elected Superintendent of San Francisco City Schools in 1902, a post which he filled until his election as District Attorney in 1905. Therefore, in May of 1911, William Langdon readily accepted the appointment offered him by Governor Johnson, to serve as a trustee for the new Fresno State Normal School. This involved selecting the site for and organizing what later would become Fresno State College. Then, in 1913, he was one of seven persons appointed by the Governor to form the first California State Board of Education and was immediately elected president of that Board. The third Johnson appointment, a judgeship, came later.

And so, during the years from 1911 to 1915, we find the Langdon home occupied by a thriving, growing family. William Langdon was commuting to San Francisco, Fresno, and Sacramento, as well as conducting business in Modesto, and opened a local law practice according to Merl McHenry. Meanwhile, wife Myrtie was involved in community and social affairs. On February 2, 1911, the Mansion was again the setting for a party, this time honoring a house guest of neighbor Eva Mae McMahon, when "the spacious parlors were prettily decorated for the event," to quote the *Stanislaus Evening News*. Entertainment included cards and a musical program "rendered at intervals throughout the evening." Besides her involvement with the building of the McHenry Library, Myrtie McHenry-Langdon was also active in the Women's Improvement Club. Earlier, in 1909, she had been one of the three members successfully requesting that the city close Wright Street, which at that time bisected Graceada Park. In April of 1912, she was elected to serve as one of the organization's four trustees, at a meeting during which it was stated that the planting of trees had been completed in Graceada Park, along the "boulevard." However, it was reported that some of the newly planted trees had been ruined by picnickers who had tied up their horses to the stakes. By 1912, the Women's Improvement Club had been responsible for the development of four Modesto parks, including Graceada and Enslen. In June of that year, Myrtie Langdon furnished one of the five automobiles that carried members on a tour around the county to promote their annual fund-raising Fiesta.

Merl McHenry was the host at a party held on the lawn of the Langdon house on April 29, 1912. The event honored the fifth birthday of his cousin, Miss Anita Conneau of San Francisco, and refreshments were served on a table set up outdoors, using a theme of "pink." There were little pink baskets at each plate, and the ice cream and cake were also pink. "The youngsters had a merry afternoon," said the *Modesto Morning Herald*. This was one of the few Mansion parties held outdoors, probably because entertaining outside during Modesto's early years was sometimes unpleasant due to hordes of mosquitos. The problem was not alleviated until the formation of the Modesto Mosquito Abatement Control District in 1945.

The home was the setting for another wedding on January 21, 1913 when Myrtie's sister, Lena Conneau, was married to George Nelson. The ceremony was held in the drawing room, in front of the fireplace, and the *Modesto Morning Herald's* description of the home decorated for the wedding is of special interest.

> The service was read by the Rev. H. K. Pitman of the Presbyterian church, and the ceremony was performed in the drawing room which was most effectively decorated, carrying out a color scheme in which the lavender and pink motif predominated. The mantle which formed the background for the bridal party was banked with ferns and roses, while streamers of lavender tulle and smilax extended to the chandelier formed a very dainty canopy. Enchantress carnations and asparagus ferns were used throughout the living room and library.
>
> Following the ceremony, dinner was served from two artistically decorated oval tables. The bride's table was covered with a beautiful drawn work cloth over a lavender pad, having a center piece of orchids and lilies of the valley. Lavender ribbons were draped from the chandelier to each cover. Place cards were heart shaped with a miniature bride on each one and the favors were small silver baskets of lavender flowers. The appointments of the other table were the same except that the color scheme was in pink.

Only immediate family members were present at the wedding, after which the newlyweds left on the evening train for San Francisco, where they boarded a boat for Los Angeles. The groom was employed by the Union Savings Bank. Lena and George Nelson soon built a home on the corner of 16th and I Streets, opposite the McMahon house. By this time the Bertram home was on the southeasterly corner of 15th and I, and the two story James Apartments, built in 1912, were located on the south corner diagonally across from the Mansion.

Myrtie and William Langdon became secondtime parents on April 15, 1913 with the arrival of nine pound Lawton William, born at the Mansion. Now Lois was three and Merl was ten. Although it was announced that the Langdon family would be spending the summer of 1913 in their Alameda home, they probably were present to watch Modesto's Fourth of July parade, because William Langdon was the Grand Marshall. Their return from a trip to Lake Tahoe in July also made the news, because they were able to make the journey by automobile from Tahoe to Modesto in 11 hours.

The grand opening of the new Hotel Modesto at the corner of 11th and H Streets created much excitement in town on June 18, 1914. A banquet and dance were held, planned by the Chamber of Commerce, and Mr. and Mrs. W.H. Langdon were among the 200 in attendance.

"Master" Merl McHenry hosted another party at the Langdon home on Halloween night of 1914. Halloween games were played until a late hour when, as described by the *Modesto Morning Herald*, "a delicious collation was served in the spacious dining room where an effective color scheme of orange and black was carried out. A huge pumpkin face was the centerpiece from which yellow ribbons led to the places for the guests." The menu included individual pumpkin pies. By this time Merl also had his own playhouse, built for him by his step-father and located directly behind the big house.

The Mansion in about 1915, with trellises across the front.

Myrtie McHenry and her children are pictured, L. to R.: Merl McHenry, Lawton Langdon, Myrtie, and Lois Langdon.

William Langdon's friend, Governor Hiram Johnson, came to Modesto at least three times during these years. Once was in 1912, when he was the vice presidential candidate running with former President Teddy Roosevelt, representing the Progressive ("Bull Moose") Party. The election was won by Democrat Woodrow Wilson. Johnson again spoke in Modesto in 1914, to an audience of 2000 on behalf of his reelection as California Governor, and also in 1916 when he was a candidate for the United States Senate. He was victorious in both of the latter campaigns. Perhaps he came to town even more often, since family members and others have said that he visited in the Langdon home on a number of occasions. At the same time, William Langdon was being approached to run for political office, particularly Congress, which he declined, noting that he was very busy with ranching and business interests. But, when Modesto's growth necessitated the formation of a second Superior Court, he accepted the appointment as Judge of Stanislaus County Superior Court #2, made by Governor Johnson. By now he had resigned from the school board positions, and he dissolved his law partnership in San Francisco at the time of the judgeship appointment in August of 1915. A newspaper biography noted that the new judge was president of the Langdonmerl Company (a realty holding company engaged in "lands, loans, stocks and bonds" according to Modesto City Directories), was engaged in farming, was president of the Suburban Residence Company with land interests in Fresno and Riverside Counties, and was vice-president of the G.P. Schafer Company. An upstairs hall in the Schafer building was renovated to become the Langdon courtroom, and on September 17 Judge and Mrs. Langdon entertained the staffs of the county newspapers and local members of the Bar at a dinner held at the Hotel Hughson. The hit of the evening, according to the *Modesto Morning Herald*, was the appearance of two of the Langdon children in costume, Lois Ann representing the press by wearing a paper dress made from various county newspapers, and Merl clad in cap, gown, and scroll to represent the law.

The memories of Merl McHenry, as revealed during several interviews, were of great assistance in piecing together the Mansion story during this period. He recalled many interesting details, such as: the barn was a long, white building with stalls, topped by a weathervane that was later placed on the house; servants always included an upstairs maid and a cook; the servants lived in the basement, except for some of the women who stayed upstairs; his pool table was in the basement room located directly under the front parlor; the house was heated by steam radiators, with a coal-burning furnace in the basement that he often stoked; his playhouse cost about $250; the house had a dumb waiter and a laundry chute; and when he was small he sometimes sat on his mother's lap while she, as Bank president, signed First National Bank notes. Other members of the family, as well as Merl, have described the "cozy corner", which was tucked away behind the front stairway near the entrance. Here were Indian rugs, baskets, and a painted Indian head on a pedestal. When he was naughty, Merl was sometimes threatened with the fierce looking Indian ("the Indian will get you!"), which "frightened him to death", he said.

We are also fortunate to have personal reminiscences by two Modestans who, as young girls, worked at the McHenry house, about three years apart. Esther Osterberg Smith did the cooking at the Mansion, while her cousin took care of the house and waited on the table, for a year in about 1911 to 1912. During an interview, Mrs. Smith shared many remembrances. She stated that the Langdons had a car and chauffeur, Mrs. Langdon had her own electric car, and there was also a gardener. The house was on a big lot with a large barn and many orange trees. The Langdons gave "political parties with people from Sacramento", for which they had a black woman come in to do the cooking, with Esther Smith then doing the serving. The kitchen had a wood stove and a work table in the middle of the room. Mrs. Langdon prepared the daily menus and ordered the food by telephone from Schafers store, which then delivered the groceries to the house. The two cousins shared a room upstairs facing I Street, and they often took care of baby Lois, particularly when the Langdons were out. She especially remembered taking Lois for walks to town, pushing her in an elaborate baby buggy which looked just like a miniature carriage with a wooden horse, "reins and all". She recalled that Lena Conneau lived in the house during this time, and in the summer the two cousins went with the family to Santa Cruz where they spent several months.

Clara Bridges Medlin worked for the Langdons as "second girl" in about 1915-16, when she was only 16 years old. She remembered a French governess who took care of the children and spoke French to them. There was also a handyman-chauffeur and a Chinese cook. She recalled that one day the cook became angry and chased her with a butcher knife until Mrs. Langdon intervened and told him to get back in the kitchen. Her duties included serving dinner, also sometimes serving lunch, picking and arranging flowers, and she used to take the newspaper to Judge Langdon. He was usually in his office, to the left of the front door, or sometimes in the library. Her room was on the second floor, at the back of the house towards the orange grove. The Langdons' bedroom was in the center, overlooking the grove, and when it was hot in the summer they used to sleep on the sleeping porch down the hall. They spent a lot of time in the upstairs sitting room, which was on the corner "and got a lot of sun". There were parties at the house, for which Mrs. Langdon and her sisters sometimes ordered dresses or gowns from San Francisco. Lena Nelson, the sister who lived across the street, was frequently at the house for dinner. Clara Medlin also recalled one summer when she spent a month in San Francisco with Mrs. Langdon and the children. They lived in a house, and the French governess and the chauffeur also went along. Her memories of Myrtie Langdon were positive. "I am glad that I got to live there with Mrs. Langdon, because she was so sweet and treated me like one of the family", she said.

Judge Langdon was victorious in his bid for reelection as Superior Court Judge in 1916 and the following year was appointed by the new Governor, William Stephens, to membership on the State Colonization Board. This was another new agency, formed to administer the Land Settlement Act passed by the legislature, and the members served without compensation. By now the country was rapidly moving towards World War I, which had started in Europe in 1914. On April 6, 1917, the United States declared war on Germany, and five months later Judge William Langdon played a role in Modesto's ceremonial send-off to the community's first draftees. Stanislaus County's initial draft quota was 20 men, and on the evening of September 5 the draftees assembled at the corner of 10th and I Streets. Escorted by the police chief, the Home Guard Companies, and the Modesto Band, they marched down 10th to H Street and then to Courthouse Park. There they were honored by several thousand citizens at a ceremony that included music by the band and a choir, patriotic singing, and an address by Judge Langdon who, in closing, said,

> And now, young men, as chairman of the Stanislaus County Council of Defense, and on behalf of all your fellow citizens of this County, I extend to you the good wishes, the gratitude, and the love of all our people. May God be with you, watch over you, and bring you home speedily, safely, and sound. Goodbye and God bless you.

The Langdon speech, described as "impressive", was printed in its entirety in the *Modesto Morning Herald.*

Finally, in December 1918, when Modesto, like the rest of the country, was suffering from an influenza epidemic, Judge Langdon was notified that he had been appointed by Governor Stephens to be presiding justice of the newly created second division of the First District Court of Appeals. "The distinguished jurist is confined to his bed with the flu and was unable to read the many congratulatory telegrams which were received here from all parts of the state", said the *Modesto Morning Herald,* adding that he had accepted the appointment. The new position was to begin in San Francisco on January 1, 1919, and Judge Langdon announced that the family would continue to maintain both of their homes, in Modesto and Alameda. He also stated that the family's business interests in Modesto would, in the future, be handled by his brother-in-law, George Nelson.

Merl McHenry remained in Modesto for his last year at the newly built Modesto High School in 1919-1920. He stayed with his aunt and uncle, Lena and George Nelson, who lived near the Mansion on the corner of 16th and I Streets (where the Stanislaus County Library is today). By then, the rest of the Langdon family had moved to Alameda, and Merl joined them on weekends in his new car. Judge Langdon had taken him to San Francisco's "auto row" and purchased for Merl the automobile of his choice, which was a Stutz Bearcat. Now, according to Merl, the McHenry-Langdon home stood empty, as another period in its long history drew to a close. However, the Langdon clan gathered in Modesto again on June 11, 1920, when Merl graduated from high school. He was awarded the coveted Plato Medal for high scholarship which was presented by Sol P. Elias, nephew of donor G.D. Plato and Modesto's historian and future mayor. During the ceremony, Elias told the audience that Merl's grandfather, Robert McHenry, had been the first one to shake his hand when he had graduated from Modesto High School in its first class on the night of May 27, 1886.

Myrtie McHenry lived in the McHenry Mansion longer than anyone.

CHAPTER 7

A SUMMING UP

Judge William Langdon became an Associate Justice of the California State Supreme Court.

As we arrive at the conclusion of our story of the lives and times of the original inhabitants of the McHenry Mansion, it seems appropriate to summarize what happened to our cast of characters as the years passed.

Judge William Henry Langdon, who resided in the McHenry Mansion much of the time during a period of 11 years, served with distinction as the presiding justice of the First District Court of Appeals in San Francisco from 1919 until 1926. He then was elected to the office of Associate Justice of the California State Supreme Court for a 12 year term. In 1938, he was reelected for another 12 years and died unexpectedly of a heart attack on August 10, 1939, at age 66. Just as in the case of the two men who lived in the McHenry Mansion before him, Robert and Oramil McHenry, Judge Langdon was an extraordinary man in his accomplishments and in his contributions to society as well as to the local community.

Myrtie McHenry-Langdon lived in the McHenry Mansion longer than any family member, for 17 years from 1902 until 1919. She left the community for the Bay Area in 1919 when her husband, William Langdon, received the Appeals Court judgeship. Following his death in 1939, she moved back to Modesto and purchased a Queen Anne Victorian style home on Hughson Road, originally built for Jenny Weldy Jones. She resided there for about ten years, much of the time with her sister Lena Conneau Nelson whose husband, George, took his own life in 1941. The home was finally sold to the E.D. Thompsons in 1952, and Myrtie moved to San Mateo near her son, Merl. She died on August 18, 1959 at age 80 and is buried in the Holy Cross Cemetery in Colma, San Francisco County, next to Judge Langdon. Myrtie was known for her generosity and, through the years, financially contributed to the well being of various family members, for college educations, houses, clothing, etc. The Langdon children, Lois and Lawton, attended the University of California, and Lawton received a Bachelor of Law degree from Stanford University in 1936. He was employed by Broadway-Hale Stores in San Francisco until his death in September of 1960 at age 47. Lois, married to Ned Marr who worked for Columbia Broadcasting Systems, resided in Pasadena until her death in May of 1973 at 63 years. Merl McHenry graduated from Stanford University, where he also earned a law degree, and later obtained a Master of Business Administration from Harvard. His successful career, first in commercial and then in investment banking, in San Francisco included many years as a vice president and trust officer with Bank of America and as a partner in the investment firm of J. Barth & Company. At one time he was chairman of the Pacific Coast Stock Exchange Board of Governors. His 1930 marriage to Marcella Bricca produced two sons, Dr. Martin McHenry of Cleveland, Ohio and Dr. Malcolm McHenry of Sacramento.

In March 1921, a bold headline in the *Modesto Morning Herald* proclaimed, "Great Bald Eagle Ranch Will Be Subdivided". Noting that the size of the ranch had dwindled through the years, the article stated that, of the remaining 620 acres, 400 acres were being sold in tracts of 20, 40, and 60 acres at $400 and up per acre and would be called the "McHenry Division". Owners Robert and Albert McHenry were to retain 220 acres of fig orchard as well as all buildings, including the family residence. By now the brothers had become famous for their White Kadota figs and White Leghorn hens, which had won many prizes. In March 1941, Albert, who never married, was drowned in a boating accident at Turlock Reservoir. Bob had three marriages, the first to Marie Jane Rogers, which produced two children known to many Modestans: Ora Louise McHenry Condrey of Carmel and Bobbe Jean McHenry Pauley Pagen of Beverly Hills. Both were born at the Bald Eagle Ranch. His other two wives were Katherine Jones (one child, Robert Wesley McHenry) and Edna Carlson (three children: Rayfield Albert McHenry, Thomas Harold McHenry who died in 1984, and Jack Robert McHenry). Bob finally left Modesto and moved to Eureka, where he died on September 16, 1946 at age 59. He is buried in Eureka. Louise Bilicke McHenry, the mother of Bob and Albert and divorced from Oramil McHenry in 1902, was remarried in 1907 to hotelier James C. Babcock. Babcock was lost at sea in 1910. She lived in San Francisco and, during her later years, spent considerable time in Modesto with her sons at the Bald Eagle Ranch until her death in January 1930. Louise's brother, Albert C. Bilicke, became very wealthy and, in fact, was reported in a local news item to have given his wife 1.5 million dollars as a Christmas present in 1912. He lost his life on board the ship Lusitania when it was torpedoed and sunk by the Germans in 1915. At that time he was the financial guardian for Bob and Albert, under the terms of Ora McHenry's will, and following the accident was legally replaced by George Stoddard until the sons reached age 28.

Albert Bilicke, who went down on the Lusitania in 1915, was Oramil McHenry's brother-in-law. The photo is from Ora Louise McHenry Condrey.

Many of these persons with whom we have become well acquainted in this story are buried in the Acacia (Masonic) Memorial Cemetery on Scenic Drive in Modesto. In 1940, Myrtie Conneau McHenry-Langdon purchased 10 graves in lot 1, block 11 for $250, which are now occupied by six adult members of the Conneau clan plus several infants. These are: the parents, F.E. Conneau, 1822-1886, and Annie Conneau, 1848-1910; daughter Matilda Conneau Schafer (the first baby girl born in Modesto), 1872-1948; daughter Lena Conneau Nelson, who in 1913 was married in the McHenry Mansion, 1885-1978; son Arthur Ernest Conneau, known as Ernie, 1880-1952; and Lena Schafer Maze Jaggard, daughter of Matilda, 1894-1981. The infant graves are unmarked. Letitia (Letty) Conneau, divorced in 1913 from Frank Cressey, Jr. and later remarried to John Havilland, died of cancer in San Mateo in May 1959 and is buried in the Golden Gate National Cemetery near San Bruno.

The McHenry Monument (see Chapter 3) is located about 100 feet west of the Conneau graves in the Acacia Memorial Cemetery and is engraved with four names: Robert McHenry 1827-1890; Matilda McHenry 1838-1896; their son Oramil McHenry 1861-1906; and his first wife, Louise E. (Bilicke McHenry) Babcock 1867-1930. But three other family members are also buried here, in unmarked graves: Albert, who drowned in 1941; Ora Louise who died of burns at age nine in 1901; and baby Russell who died at six and a half months in 1896.

This completes our story of the original families that lived in the McHenry Mansion. However, it doesn't end the history of the house, which moved into a commercial phase that lasted for over 50 years.

Annie Conneau, mother of Myrtie, is buried near her husband and several of her children in the Masonic (Acacia) Cemetery on Scenic Drive.

CHAPTER 8

THE ELMWOOD SANITARIUM

The McHenry-Langdon home had a new name by 1920. It was called the Elmwood Sanitarium. The manager was Royal W. Hammond, who lived in the house with his family.

The facility was one of a number of sanitariums in operation throughout the country at this time under the auspices of the Seventh Day Adventist Church. The Battle Creek Systems, mentioned in the above advertisement, referred to a type of medical treatment featured at the famous Battle Creek Sanitarium in Michigan. It was based on the use of therapy by physical agents, such as hydrotherapy, combined with diet and other measures including exercise. The Battle Creek Sanitarium was directed by Dr. John Harvey Kellogg in the late 1880s, who also invented peanut butter, grain and nut food products, and the cereal breakfast foods that today bear his name.

The Elmwood Sanitarium at 906 15th Street functioned very quietly. Several neighbors of the day say that there was no sign on the building, and even the newspaper advertisements did not give its location. However, the Modesto City Directories of 1919-1922 identified the Elmwood Sanitarium by name and address. The listing during those years read, "Elmwood Sanitarium, R.W. Hammond mgr., Battle Creek Methods, I cr 15th, tel. 796". One of the few original McHenry items in the house, a desk, has an "Elmwood Sanitarium" stamp on the lower left drawer. This oak desk, which also has "A. McHenry" written in pencil on the lower right drawer, was in the possession of Ora Louise McHenry Condrey who donated it to the Mansion.

The memories of three Modestans add to this story of the Sanitarium. Isabel Warren Hartwich, who as a child lived across the street on 15th, played with Hazel Hammond, the young daughter of the manager. She stated that the children were admonished to play quietly in the house, because there were "sick people" there. Longtime Modesto resident Rosamond Raynor Flygare visited an ill friend who was being treated as an in-patient at the Elmwood Sanitarium. According to Mrs. Flygare, two physicians associated with the Sanitarium were Dr. John Muncey Bulpitt and his wife, Dr. Zoe Nightingale Bulpitt, with offices first in the Black Building (at 1115 I Street) and later at 908 11th Street. Mrs. Flygare was also an obstetrical patient of Dr. John Bulpitt, who delivered her baby at St. Mary's Hospital on H Street. That institution later became Modesto City Hospital. Another Modestan with memories of the Elmwood Sanitarium is Paul H. Smith, whose father, Armour B. Smith, was a patient at the facility in 1920. The senior Smith was suffering from sciatica, (a painful irritation of the sciatic nerve extending from the low back into the leg) and remained for a month in the Sanitarium. Young Paul, who was attending Modesto High School at the time, stayed with his father every night and slept in the same room. During an interview, he recalled that the patient was bedridden and was given treatments, such as hot towel applications. The physicians were Drs. Bulpitt and Bulpitt, both of whom were usually present during the evening, with Dr. Zoe Bulpitt mostly administering the treatments. The Smiths were in the upstairs

South room (the McHenrys' former sitting room), and there seemed to be patients in all of the second floor rooms as well as many downstairs. Nurses were also in evidence. Paul Smith's impression was that the Elmwood Sanitarium was a very busy place.

Further investigation of the Bulpitts has revealed that they received their medical degrees from the College of Medical Evangelists in Los Angeles, which in 1961 became the Loma Linda University School of Medicine. Dr. Zoe Bulpitt graduated in 1914 and her husband in 1918. The Sanitarium continued to operate at 906 15th Street until 1923, when the Langdons converted the house into apartments. At that time, the Elmwood Sanitarium moved to 304 McHenry Avenue, still operated by Royal Hammond. But by 1924, the Sanitarium and Hammond were no longer listed in the Modesto City Directory and, according to Mrs. Flygare, the Bulpitts had moved to Santa Ana, California.

CHAPTER 9

THE APARTMENT HOUSE

On Saturday, October 6, 1923, the McHenry Mansion was viewed by the public for the first time in its new role of "apartment house". The apartments, which were "constructed from the Langdon residence" according to a news item, were open for inspection from 2 to 6 p.m. on that date. Contractor George J. Ulrich was in charge of the remodeling, which had taken nearly four months. An announcement of the proposed conversion of the house into apartments had been made by Judge William Langdon in June, when the *Modesto Morning Herald* noted that "one of Modesto's beautiful residences is to be converted into a high class aparment house". Some of Ulrich's comments about the project, as quoted in the *Herald* on October 3, 1923, are of interest.

> No expense has been spared to make these apartments equal to the best that may be found in the great metropolitan centers. Comfort, convenience, beauty, and location make these distinctive and non-competitive. Sweeping lawns, beautiful flowers, and producing orange groves make a setting unique and unusual for apartments here or elsewhere. There are eleven homelike, completely and newly furnished apartments, consisting each of a large, cool living room, kitchenette and bath. Large individual storage lockers for trunks and other articles are provided in the attic and basement. A vapor heating system has been installed. Hot and cold water service is available day and night. Gas for cooking and electricity for lighting are metered to each apartment. Janitor service is provided. The apartments are designed to meet the needs of an ever increasing class who wish to escape the burdens of a large house with its attendant domestic help problem and who desire the privacy, freedom and home atmosphere unattainable in a hotel. These apartments make an especial appeal to all who believe that beautiful home surroundings contribute greatly to the joy of living.

The remodeling was extensive and included the construciton of many interior walls, closing off original doorways and opening up others, and the addition of a central hall. Three sun porches were added to the exterior of the building, and the front veranda was enclosed to provide more space for the front apartments. New plumbing, wiring, and a heating system were installed, and each of the 11 apartments had its own bathroom and kitchenette. According to former residents, every unit was provided with a stove, a small "ice box", a built-in kitchen table or booth, mirrors, and a bed that pulled down out of the wall.

upper left:
The Hyland Goulds converted the large third floor attic into an apartment. This photo was taken in 1977, after the building was donated to the city.

upper right:
The second floor sun porch had a fine view of the town.

lower left:
The cupola as viewed from the third floor apartment.

Thus by late 1923, the home at 906 15th Street had become the Langdon Apartments and was open for business. For the next 49 years, from 1923 until 1972, the McHenry Mansion was operated as an apartment house and had several owners. The house remained in the McHenry-Langdon family until October 1936, when it was sold to Hyland Hicks (Hy) Gould and his wife Hildagard for $20,000. The sale included the house and the ten lots originally purchased by Robert McHenry in the 1880s. The next owners, in 1952, were James H. and Alice M. Boulton. They paid $47,000 for the house and four lots, the site comprising 100 feet on 15th and 140 feet on I Street. Finally, in April 1954, Luther W. Crabtree bought the house and the four lots, #17-#20 in block #122, for $55,000. Crabtree maintained the building as an apartment house until 1972 and after that as a family residence until his death in 1975.

The first manager of the Langdon Apartments was Gustav H. Bertram, the neighbor who, since 1904, had lived across the street on the south corner of 15th and I. Bertram at that time was also president of the Peoples Finance and Thrift Company, and he and his wife, Palmira, managed the Langdon Apartments for several years. By 1934 Carl F. Shirk and then George C. Nelson were the managers, and in 1936 the new owners, the Goulds, took over its operation. Hy Gould was also proprietor and owner of the well known Gould's Restaurant, located at 921 I Street. Gould died in June 1943, and Mrs. Gould later married John D. Leonard and left the community. Samuel W. Smith then managed the building, probably until the Boultons took possession. From 1954 until 1972, the apartments were operated by Vera Vecherok Crabtree and Luther Crabtree. The house had three names during its long aparment period: the Langdon Apartments, Gould Apartments, and Crabtree Apartments. The Boultons apparently did not change the building's name during their short tenure as landlords.

Although the house was originally divided into 11 apartments, the third floor and the basement were later remodeled into additional units, totaling 14 apartments. It was the Hyland Goulds who closed in the large, unfinished third floor attic and converted it into an apartment. Referred to as the "penthouse", this is where the Goulds themselves lived. According to former friends and family, the apartment was elegantly furnished, decorated with white carpets, rich satins, and pastel toned French Provincial furniture. The floor of the cupola was removed, and balconies were built on the bays that extended from each side of the house. The only access to the third floor was by the back stairway, of which the third flight was especially steep. Friends reportedly referred to the Gould's penthouse apartment as the "panthouse", because they were panting by the time they ascended the steep stairs. Eventually, there was a second very small apartment on the third floor identified as #12a, added by Luther Crabtree. Crabtree also developed the basement apartment that became #14 and, through the years, did extensive re-wiring, painting, carpeting, and renovating.

By interviewing a number of the Modestans who lived in the apartments, it has been possible to put together a picture of life in the Mansion as a tenant. "It was fun", was the frequent comment by former residents. People remember it as a cheerful, pleasant place to live, with many of the rooms well-windowed and sunny. They liked the high ceilings, the handsome front staircase, the old chandeliers, and several mentioned the tall claw-foot bathtubs. Early residents enjoyed looking out at the orange grove and receiving a box of oranges at Christmas. They recalled viewing the Fourth of July parades from the side porch or from their own apartment windows. "Safe" was a term commonly used to describe living in the apartments, important because many of the residents were single women. Some who worked in downtown offices didn't own cars and walked everywhere, a particular advantage during the World War II years when gasoline was rationed. They grocery-shopped at Piggly-Wiggly on 10th, H and J Streets; at Mellis Brothers on I; and in later years at the Home Market at 12th and J and at Justesen's on J near 14th. Special dining spots were Taza's Tea Room on 12th Street and the Hotel Modesto at 11th and I, with other favorite restaurants at the Hotel Hughson, the Hotel Covell during a later period, and Gould's. The apartments were just a block from the McHenry Library and less than three blocks from the "show" at the State Theater on J Street, where adult tickets cost 25 cents in the 1930s. Other movie theaters were recalled with fondness: the Strand and Lyric on 10th and the Princess (later the Covell) on J. Former residents remembered walking downtown to Modesto's main shopping street, which was 10th, where they usually met friends and could

clockwise:
Some of the former residents mentioned the tall claw-foot bathtubs.

The apartments had high ceilings, some of the original chandeliers, and steam heat. This one was on the second floor. Photo was taken 1976.

Another second floor apartment.

View of the top of the staircase during the apartment era.

Residents admired the handsome front staircase and the newell post. Note the wall to the left of the stairway, which had been added. It was removed during the restoration.

91

MODESTO MORNING HERALD
December 25, 1923

buy almost everything. On 10th Street, at various times, were department stores called Latz's, Shackelford-Ullman Company, Loeb's, J.C. Penney, Montgomery Ward, and Sears Roebuck; men's wear at Plato's, Musser's, the Toggery, Dozier & Leiter, and J.S. Williams; women's wear at Kelly's, Hammett's, and Priester's Town Shop; drug stores named Maze, Modesto, Central, Longs, and Thrifty; variety stores such as S.H. Kress, F.W. Woolworth, and J.J. Newberry; shoes at Sutton's Slipper Shoppe, Browne's, and Coey's Wonder Shoe Store; ladies' hats at Dunning Millinery; bakery goods at Carnation Bakery; and newspapers and magazines at Nichol News.

A number of school teachers were among the first renters, in the 1920s, when the Langdon Apartments were young (as well as the teachers). These included Alice Cooper, Dorothy Eakin, Marguerite Johnson, Lulu Moorehead, Adeline Rosebrock, Nellie Scott, Washington School Principal Elsie Turner, and Modesto Junior College teachers Jessie Kline, Edna Barr Love, and Mary Aline Polk. Other early residents, dating to 1924, were attorney Thomas Boone and Schafer's store manager Ed Hunsucker, with his wife Catherine.

Some tenants remained for a short time, until a residence somewhere else was completed or vacated. An example were newlyweds Ernest and Wilma Brysan who, in October 1928, stayed just six weeks before moving to Merced. Their rent was $22.50 per month. Others lived there for many years. The longevity record undoubtedly belongs to Norma F. Norberto who resided at 906 15th Street for 26 years, from October 1946 until it was closed in 1972. Her apartment was #9 on the second floor, in the center of the building facing I Street. It had a large living room, kitchen, bath, a sleeping porch, and an outside porch where she raised house plants. Employed at Lee's Apparel shop, which was on I Street between 10th and 11th and later on J at 17th, she was able to walk to work and even go home for lunch. Apartment #9 rented for $40 a month in 1946 and $95 by the 1970s.

Matilda Conneau Schafer, older sister of Myrtie Conneau McHenry-Langdon and the wife of merchant George Schafer, lived in the apartment house for 20 years, beginning in about 1927. Widowed in 1923, she moved into apartment #1 following the sale of the Schafer home at 1104 15th Street. Her apartment was the original front parlor, located to the right of the entrance on the first floor. Other residents such as Norma Norberto and Mary Aline Polk recalled sitting on the front porch in the evenings with "Tillie" Schafer, listening to her talk about the town's early days and the parties in the McHenry house.

Another 20 year tenant was Bessie Silverthorn, head librarian of the McHenry Library, whose tenure began in 1933. It is said that she lived on the first floor in the middle apartment facing I Street, which was #3. Lourinda Hickey was a 15 year resident, from 1957 to 1972, in apartment #2 located at the left of the front door on the first floor. Some shared an apartment, such as three young women who lived in the basement (#14) for about five months in 1966, named Linda Houston, Charlene Deve, and Vicki Waters. Their furnished apartment had seven rooms, with a large living room, formal dining room, a den, two bedrooms, kitchen and bath, and rented for $110. Alice Fitts and Peggy Palmer lived in the penthouse in 1948-1949, and Alice particularly recalled receiving her engagement ring from Claude Kenworthy on the stair landing. Ex-penthouse dwellers commented on their discomfort during the warm summers, which caused some to sleep outside on the small balconies.

Two memorable events were mentioned by a number of former residents who lived in the Crabtree Apartments in the 1960s. One was the theft of a large oil painting, original to the house, that hung in the entrance lobby. It happened one night in the spring of 1966, according to William and Betty Nichols who lived in the basement apartment. She heard scuffling sounds on the floor above at about 9:30 o'clock, when the crime occurred. The painting, which was four by eight feet in a heavy gold leaf frame, was painted by Alfred C. Rodriguez of San Francisco and was valued at $2000. The tenants were relieved when Derald Crabtree, Luther's son who operated the family's Town House Lodge next door to the apartments, received an anonymous telephone call. He was told that the painting had been left at Graceada Park. The Crabtrees found it at the south end of the park, only slightly damaged.

The second happening had to do with a fire. Several tenants, including Norma Norberto, were outside the building when they noticed smoke pouring out from a second floor window on the I Street side. High schooler Elaine Crabtree ran into the house and pounded on doors to rout the residents. When the firemen arrived and climbed a ladder to get in through the window, they discovered that the fire and smoke were coming from a barbecue which was being used, illegally, to cook steaks in the apartment.

Ironically, it was the threat of fire that finally led to the closing of the Crabtree Apartments in 1972. In September of that year, city inspectors stated that the apartment house was in violation of Modesto's Dangerous Buildings code. They ordered the installation of a number of fire safety improvements, if the building were to continue as an apartment house. These included the addition of modern stairway-type fire escapes to the upper floors, enclosed interior stairwells, changes in the exit doors, and fire-resistive walls and ceilings in the basement. Stating that the cost of such renovation would be prohibitive, the Crabtrees gave a month's notice to the eight tenants. Now, once again the house became a private residence, this time for Crabtree family members.

The McHenry Mansion was not in the news again until 1975, when Luther Crabtee died on August 1 at age 87. It was soon announced that the Mansion was for sale, with several possibilities mentioned. At least one group was reported to be interested in converting the house into a restaurant, and the idea of making the building into a community art center was proposed. The assessed valuation of the house was listed at $83,000, although it was suggested that it would probably sell for much more.

Thus by early 1976, an important question being asked in the community was, "What is going to happen to the McHenry Mansion"?

This painting, which was hung in the entrance lobby, was stolen in 1966.

THE APARTMENT ERA

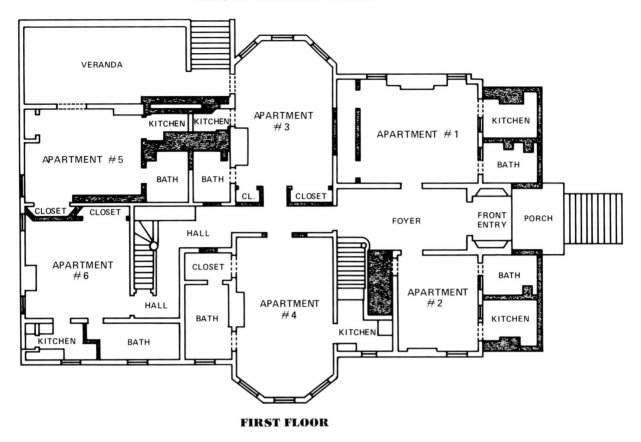

FIRST FLOOR

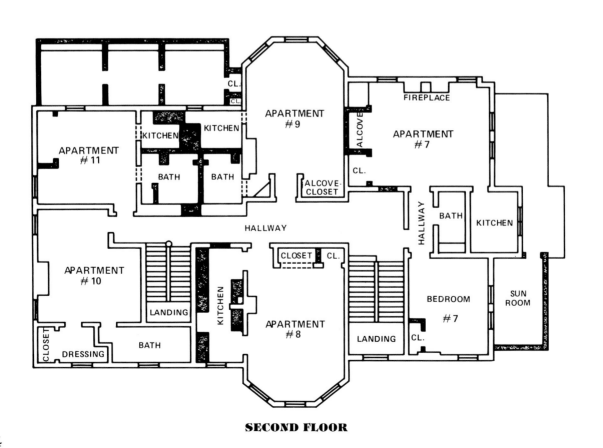

SECOND FLOOR

94

THE APARTMENT DWELLERS

The following are some of the residents of the Langdon-Gould-Crabtree Apartments from 1923 to 1972. The names were gathered from interviews and word-of-mouth reports, from many responses to newspaper articles requesting such information, and from city directories. The names are listed by decade and, where they are known, women's current married names are given in parentheses. Since the dates of residence and spellings of some of the names are dependent upon people's memories of events that happened many years ago, there may be a few misspellings and date errors, for which the author appologizes.

1920s

Abbott, J.W.
Barth, Ethyl
Boone, Thomas C.
Brown, Ressie
Brysan, Ernest & Wilma
Conley, William J.
Cooper, Alice

Eakin, Dorothy (Bagley)
Grollman, Therese (Taza)
Hunsucker, Ed E. & Catherine
Johnson, Marguerite (Price)
Kline, Jessie M.
Love, Edna Barr
Matthewson, Helen (Miller)

McNeil, Sarah D.
Moorehead, Lulu (Ryan)
Polk, Mary Aline
Rosebrock, Adeline
Schafer, Matilda C.
Scott, Nellie
Turner, Elsie V.
Turrell, Joanne

1930s

Archibald, Hedley C.
Ashton, Phillip
Black, Charles and Kay
Boyle, Leonard and Nita
Boone, Thomas C.
Cornell, Samuel V.
Danner, Peggy
Dexter, Carrie B.
Duncan, Charles H.
Eakin, Dorothy (Bagley)
Esgar, Reese and Zola

Evans, Virginia M.
Ferguson, Bessie
Gould, Hyland & Hildagard
Green, Louis H. & Helen
High, James V.
Lorang, Mrs. Jake
Love, Edna Barr
Mendell, Winnifred
Monroe, Lester & Dorothy
Platt, Laura (Arnold)
Platt, Mollie Starks

Polk, Mary Aline
Price, Alicous & Jessica
Ryan, Thomas and Lulu
Schafer, Matilda C.
Shirk, Carl and Lelia
Silverthorn, Bessie
Smiley, Thomas & Estella
Townsend, Lolita
Wade, William & Helen
Wilbur, Harold R.
Wilbur, W.B.

1940s

Achterberg, Peggy (De Freest)
Bradford, Clarkson, Jr. & Marian
Brady, Lanier & Miriam
Brooks, Barbara (Inglis)
Brooks, Jack & Lorrine
Caldwell, William
Carroll, Maynard & Edna
Castleman, Beatrice (Shamlin)
Cox, James and Peggy
Cummins, Dorothy
Fitts, Alice (Kenworthy)
Garlock, J.L. and Bess
Gould, Hyland and Hildagard
Harbaugh, Wellington
Horton, Benjamin W.
Jeffers, Lillian

Jeffers, Zola
Jones, Josephine
Knott, John
Kuykendall, William & Dorothy
Lee, Mary
Magladry, Mrs. Grover
May, Louise
Norberto, Norma
O'Leary, Peggy
Palmer, Margaret (Woodruff)
Polk, Mary Aline
Pritchard, Joyce
Ringelman, Katherine
Ryan, Thomas F.
Schafer, Matilda C.
Scharnberg, Harold & Harriett

Scharnberg, Sally (Melford)
Scharnberg, William & Mary
Schmitt, Anne E.
Schmitt, Delano & Grace
Silverthorn, Bessie
Smith, Samuel & Stella
Smith, Virginia
Strunk, Barbara
Strunk, Rudolf
Summerhouse, William
Taylor, Ruby
Thompson, Ardel
Tredway, J.R.
Turner, Paul and Raylene
Webber, Genevieve (Simms)
Wilbur, H.R.

1950s

Abel, Morris Mitchell
Abbott, Floyd and Virginia
Beastrom, Beverly
Beeson, Edward A. and Blanche
Bengston, Beverly
Borland, Helen
Bradley, James
Crabtree, Derald and Dorothy
Creasy, Leslie M.
Davis, Mrs. Sael T.
De Yoe, Lillian
Eastham, Roxie
Esgar, Reese and Zola
Foster, F.B.
Garcia, Leo
George, Grace
Haveiler, Donald
Hickey, Lourinda

Kuykendall, William & Dorothy
Maclusi, Beverly
Manross, Beulah (Nichols)
Marlow, Nora
Miedema, Gerald
Miller, Arthur
Monaco, Renee
Morey, Elaine
Nance, Floyd and Dorothy
Navajar, A. and Mary
Nelson, Natalie
Norberto, Norma F.
Orville, M. Dick
Parker, Mary D.
Peterson, Frank
Posterick, Mary
Quinn, Phyllis
Robertson, Lee

Salter, Richard
Scheider, Carol
Silverthorn, Bessie
Smith, Maude H.
Smith, Samuel
Snyder, Carol
Stienne, Beverly
Storm, Adda B.
Stryinga, Lucy R.
Taylor, Robert B.
Trip, Ethel
Werner, Charles
Whitmore, Robert and Edna
Whitfield, Dean
Whitte, J.B.
Wilson, Rennie
Young, Esther C.

1960s

Anderson, Suzanne
Anderson, Penny
Asher, Theodore
Aspinall, Herbert W.
Alluisi, Mae
Bosse, Doris
Bowley, Louis E.
Burkholder, Joanne
Carrigan, Mary
Clark, Beulah L.
Coburn, John C.
Corrigan, James
Crabtree, Derald and Dorothy
Crabtree, Elaine (Greydanus)
Crabtree, June (DiLallo)
Crabtree, Luther and Vera
Deve, Charlene
Dinsmore, Robert W.
Edlund, Peggy
Eiving, Belvina
Fish, Riley
Flenning, Gary and Mary
Friend, Charlene D.
Gilgoff, Lawrence
Grant, Carol

Hansen, Carol
Hawley, Ernest
Hickey, Lourinda
Houston, Linda (Bosowski)
Haveiler, Ruby
Huddleston, Joseph T.
Johnson, Calvin
Kaldahl, Alice
Karpe, Margaret
Kirtpatrick, B.N.
Lee, Stella and Orvin
Lindsey, Ruby (Lewis)
Linhares, Peter
Manross, Beulah (Nichols)
Marlow, Nora
Martin, Hazel
Miller, Arthur
Monaco, Renee
Montez, Ray and Gloria
Myers, Martha
Nichols, Beulah
Nichols, Karen
Nichols, William and Betty
Norberto, Norma
Orth, Marie (Griffin)

Park, S.E.
Peterson, S.B. and Emma
Pflaghardt, Don
Purdy, Edna
Powell, Bill
Read, Marsha
Riise, Dianne (Jennings)
Robertson, Lee
Robinson, Gigi
Romine, Sandy
Rossi, Mary
Scales, Debby
Slaughter, Dale and Lee Ann
Story, Phyllis
Stesanko, Joan (Rutschow)
Stull, Veronica
Taraska, Lucy
Thiel, Patricia (Comella)
Tibbs, Dorothy
Timberlake, Don and Linda
Tutsch, Gail J.
Waters, Vicki
Watson, Sandra
Werkheiser, Donald and Lela
Whitt, Alice

1970s

Adkins, Eleanor
Cahill, Ann
Carrigan, Mary
Crabtee, Luther and Vera
Fish, Riley
Hickey, Lourinda

Karpe, Margaret
Kellough, I.
Kilgore, Ann
Lindsey, Ruby (Lewis)
Linhares, Peter and Gita
Martin, Hazell

Martin, Owen
Norberto, Norma
Rossi, Rose M.
Sanjean, John and Illona
Saurez, Patricia
Tibbs, Dorothy
Zvigzne, Normand

CHAPTER 10

THE RESTORATION

On April 14, 1976, Julio Gallo, co-president of the E & J Gallo Winery, stood on the front steps of the McHenry Mansion and announced the good news. He stated that the Julio R. Gallo Foundation had purchased the McHenry Mansion and was donating it to the City of Modesto. The Mayor, Lee H. Davies, accepted the property on behalf of the City from Gallo and his wife, Aileen, and conducted them on a tour through the house. The Modesto City Council had earlier indicated an interest in the preservation of the Mansion, and Davies had handled the arrangements with the Gallos. It was later revealed that the purchase price for the property was $150,000, including lots #17-20. Julio Gallo noted that, through the years, he and his wife had observed the demolition of many of Modesto's original structures and "we were unwilling to see the house put to commercial use, or fall under the wrecker's hammer. So we decided to buy the fine old mansion and donate it to the citizens of the community as a lasting heritage". In accepting the gift, Mayor Davies expressed the hope that the Gallos' generous gesture would encourage others to participate in the home's restoration, adding "Your gift will assure that the McHenry Mansion will continue as a Modesto landmark and will long be remembered by the community". The Modesto City Council formally accepted the Gallo gift on April 20, which marked the beginning of the next phase of the Mansion's long history: the period of restoration.

The City Council assigned the restoration project to the Modesto Culture Commission, which was given the following Mayor's Charge:

The Modesto Culture Commission will work with City Staff and others to:

1. Develop a recommended plan for restoration of the McHenry Mansion, as nearly as feasible, to its original state.
2. Develop a recommended plan for bringing the building up to safety standards for use by the public.
3. Develop cost estimates for renovation and safety update.
4. Develop a recommended plan of uses for the building, including a recommended policy for users.

The restoration began in February 1979, with the replacement of the roof.

left to right:
This is how the front of the house looked in 1977.

One of the most dramatic of the restoration projects was the removal of the front sunporch. Here the windows have been removed.

Thus began a long-term, continuing effort, involving hundreds of dedicated citizens and thousands of hours. A call immediately went out to the community, asking for help in restoring the Mansion. Many committees were organized to develop plans in specific areas. Some were general in scope, such as the committees on Use, Research, Fund Raising, Public Relations, and a Speakers' Bureau. Others were concerned with the decoration of the house, including Furnishings, Lighting, Fireplaces and Mirrors, Wall Treatment, Window Treatment, Art in the Mansion, Kitchen, Floor Covering, Needlework, and Glassware, China and Silver. A Landscaping Committee was formed to study the development of the grounds. The work of the Use Committee was the first to be completed, and by late 1976, potential uses for the building had been determined. These were in part based on public input at several open meetings. The Modesto City Council, on the recommendation of the Culture Commission and the Use Committee, adopted the general policy that "the McHenry Mansion should be maintained as a living legacy for all of the people of Modesto to enjoy, but at the same time provide appropriate funcitons that are in keeping with the decorum and majestic appearance of the Mansion". It was decided that most of the house would be available on a rental basis for public use, the exceptions being the inaccessible third floor and three specific rooms. The "viewing only" rooms were designated as the front parlor on the first floor and two bedrooms upstairs. A number of uses were suggested for the house that, as the years have passed, proved to be realistic. These include receptions, meetings, recitals, literary events, art shows, weddings, city functions, private family reunions, educational tours, and catered brunches, lunches, and dinners. An art gallery was planned for the second floor, and the basement was assigned a variety of functions such as workshops, meetings, and restrooms that would meet the needs of the handicapped. About this time, another milestone in the Mansion's history occurred when it was placed on the *National Register of Historic Places.*

Meanwhile, other restoration committees were involved with the City Staff in planning for the layout and decoration of the house, and the Fund Raising Committee sponsored a number of money-generating events. Finally, plans were prepared and cost estimates were made by the Staff, and construction on the first phase of the renovation began in February 1979.

Wayne Mathes, the restoration consultant and Supervisor of Historical Buildings for the City of Modesto, has listed the important facets of the restoration, divided into two phases as follows:

PHASE I

Exterior restoration: roof replacement using wood shingles, removal of roof dormers and two balconies on the third floor, removal of three sun porches (two facing I Street, one on 15th) reconstruction of front porch and door to 1883 period, and reconstruction of side veranda to original Victorian Italianate style.

Interior restoration: restoration of the first floor to reconstruct the interior to its original 1883 appearance by removing all of the kitchens, baths, closets, fixtures, and interior walls that were added during the apartment remodeling; also the finding and opening up of doorways in original existing walls; decoration and furnishing in the style of the Robert McHenry period.

Lower level (basement) restoration: installation of many of the buildings support systems, restrooms meeting the needs of the handicapped, and four multipurpose rooms.

Updating of house's support systems: renovation of basic services to meet city fire and safety codes, including complete re-wiring, re-plumbing, and new heating and cooling systems; installation of fire sprinklers, smoke detector devices, and burglar alarm systems; the addition of an elevator to meet state handicap regulations.

PHASE II

Interior restoration: restoration of the second floor to its original layout; removal of all apartment walls, kitchens, baths, closets, and fixtures; opening up of doorways in original walls; decoration and furnishing mostly to the Oramil McHenry era of 1896-1906; installation of support systems as in Phase I.

Third floor or attic area: development of space to house support systems for the second floor and to provide a caretaker's apartment.

LANDSCAPING

Formulation of a landscaping plan, to include original features such as the elaborate wooden fence and the orange grove; inclusion of a reception area on the east side of the house, with the Poets' Corner incorporated as the focal point; plantings typical of the McHenry periods (1883-1906); provision for modern facilities such as parking, lighting, and service access.

By 1983, with the reconstruction making great progress and an opening date projected for late in the year, it was decided that the project needed a volunteer support group. This led to the formation of the non-profit McHenry Mansion Foundation, which today fulfills several very important roles in the operation of the house. According to its Bylaws, the general purpose of the group is to solicit, receive, and administer funds for: the restoration, furnishing and maintenance of the McHenry Mansion as a property of historical significance; and the operation and support of the docents' program of the McHenry Mansion as an educational, historical, and cultural activity. The Foundation also advises the City of Modesto regarding all aspects of the McHenry Mansion. General membership is open to everyone and today totals several hundred persons. A Board of Trustees is elected annually by the membership, with a number of committees appointed by the Board. These include Executive, Finance, and Acquisitions and Restorations Committees; a Docent and Emeritus Council; and committees on Public Relations, Development, Conservation, Programming, and Public Use. One of the first tasks of the newly organized Foundation was to plan and coordinate the grand opening of the McHenry Mansion on its 100 year anniversary. More than a thousand people attended the elegant reception held at the house on Friday, December 16, 1983, where the docents and Christmas carolers wore Victorian costumes and dignitaries arrived in a horse-drawn carriage. Open house continued for the next two days, so that the entire community could have the opportunity to see what had been happening at the Mansion. In 1984, the McHenry Mansion became available to the public, for the uses specified above and free house tours. Although facing years of further restoration, the building was once again a home, now owned and managed by the citizens of Modesto. Members of the McHenry Mansion's first governing bodies are listed in Appendix F.

This brings us to the present, with a few thoughts about the past. When Robert McHenry began the construction of his home at the corner of 15th and I Streets in the summer of 1882, he certainly could never have visualized its amazing future. Little did he know that, in the second decade of the following century, the building would be cut up into 14 apartments -- and then, in another 60 years, restored to its original state. How surprised he would have been, to learn that today his house is being preserved as one of Modesto's few remaining historical landmarks. If he were able to return and walk into his former home, what would he think? Would he approve of the sight before him? We can only guess at his answer, of course, but we do so with confidence. Yes, we think he would.

The front sunporch is off.

This is how the house looked following the porch removal.

Next came the task of eliminating the added walls on the front veranda. First the windows were removed.

Here the outer wall has been removed.

The front steps were replaced.

New redwood columns for the corner of the front veranda had to be milled. Here just one is in place.

Next the second pillar was carefully positioned.

Another interesting procedure was the removal of the porches on the I Street side. In this photo, the windows are being taken out of the upstairs sunporch.

103

left to right:
The porches are gone on the I Street side of the house.

The porches were reduced to rubble.

A new staircase is built for the I Street entrance.

This photo shows the old stairs and the new ones.

Carpenter prepares the grill for under the veranda.

The side veranda is being reconstructed.

The finished grill work is in place.

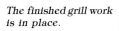

This scene is in the dining room.

A later stage in the restoration. Photo was taken in the front parlor, looking towards the back parlor.

The interior restoration is underway. This photograph was taken from the back parlor, looking into the front parlor.

When the wall next to the front staircase was removed, it opened up the stairway.

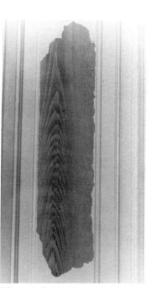

Many of the house's fireplaces were covered during the apartment era. Scraping through layers of paint and plaster revealed original colors and materials, as can be seen above the fireplace.

Scraping through the paint on doors revealed dark natural finish underneath.

Final finishing required skill and care. The craftsman graining the wood is one of only a few people now using the skills for this lost art.

THE MANSION OPENS TO THE PUBLIC

The evening of December 16, 1983 was the formal opening of the restored McHenry Mansion. This photo, looking towards the library, was taken that afternoon and illustrates the last minute preparations that were underway.

As the dusk of winter closed in, the house was ready and waiting for the guests to arrive.

Just as in Robert McHenry's day, a horse-drawn carriage was used to transport some of the guests to the Mansion.

I Street view of restored Mansion.

THE McHENRY CLAN

Robert McHenry
b.1827   d.1890
m. Matilda Hewitt
b.1838 d.1896

Oramil McHenry
b.1861   d.1906

------------- 1st m.   Louise Bilicke
b.1867 d.1930

2nd m.   Myrtie Conneau ------
b.1878   d.1959

-------- 2nd m.   William Langdon ------
b.1873   d.1939

2nd m.   James C. Babcock

Robert Albert McHenry
b.1887   d.1946

3rd m. Edna Carlson

Albert Hewitt McHenry
b.1888   d.1941

Ora Louise McHenry
b.1891   d.1901

Russell McHenry
b.1895   d.1896

Merl McHenry
b.1903
m. Marcella Bricca

Martin McHenry

Malcom McHenry

Lois Langdon
b.1910   d.1973
m. Ned Marr

Peter Marr

Michael Marr

William Marr

Hilarie Marr

Lawton Langdon
b.1918   d.1960
m. Florence Douglas

Patricia Langdon

William Langdon

2nd m. Katherine Jones

Robert Wesley McHenry

Rayfield Albert McHenry

Thomas Harold McHenry

Jack Robert McHenry

1st m. Marie Rogers

Ora Louise McHenry

Bobbie Jean McHenry

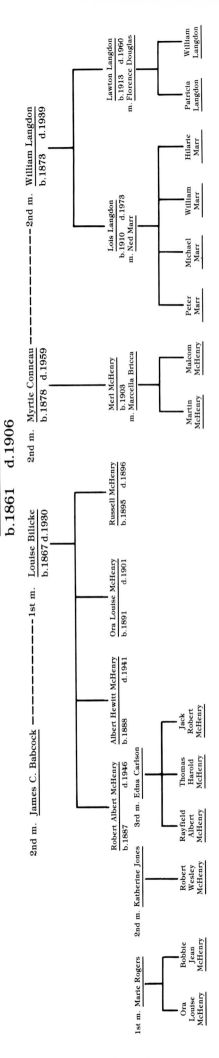

THE CONNEAU CLAN

Frank Ernest Conneau
b.1822   d.1886
m. Annie Waters
b.1848 d.1910

William Albert Conneau
b.1870   d.1930s

Matilda Conneau
b.1872   d.1948

Myrtie Conneau
b.1878   d.1959

Arthur Ernest Conneau
b.1880   d.1952

Letitia Conneau
b.1882   d.1959

Lena Conneau
b.1885 d.1978

(Note: Lena Schafer Jaggard was the daughter of Matilda Conneau and George Schafer.)

CHAPTER I
A PLACE IN HISTORY

Page 11. The Robert McHenry home was always at the top of the lists of the "finest" and most "beautiful" residences in Modesto, published in early day local newspapers. For example, an article about Modesto in the *Stanislaus County News* on February 28, 1890 stated that the "handsomest residences in the city" were owned by R. McHenry, W. Bledsoe, W.E. Turner, Y.H. Boudreau, H. Voight, and E.B. Beard. It also reported that homes in the community were valued at up to $25,000. Of the above homes, only the McHenry house stands today.

CHAPTER II
THE WORLD OF ROBERT McHENRY

Page 13. The Society of California Pioneers was established in California on September 17, 1849. It had two requirements for membership: to be a citizen of the United States, or capable of becoming one, and to be a citizen and a resident of California prior to September 9, 1850 (the day of California's admission into the Union). The Stanislaus County Chapter of the Society was organized on May 7, 1887, at a meeting held in the office of the City Clerk in Modesto.

Page 13. A number of McHenrys had located in Northern California by 1850, particularly in San Francisco, Sacramento, and Calaveras County. There were also at least two men by the name of McHenry, other than Robert, in Modesto during this period. One of the first settlers in the newly established town of Modesto in 1870 was James R. McHenry, who operated a Front Street saloon. Born in Kentucky in 1832, he was active in Democrat politics and served on the Board of Supervisors from 1867 to 1869. He moved to Yolo County in 1873 where he died in 1881, leaving a sister in Modesto according to a news item. Another McHenry, referred to only as W.S., was awarded the contract to do the grading for the construction of the Modesto Courthouse building in Modesto in 1872. But two of the most interesting early references to the name McHenry were in Stockton newspapers and directories. The *San Joaquin County Directory, 1871-1872,* had a listing for "McHenry, Robert, farmer, residence corner

Beaver and Flora, Stockton", and Stockton Directories for 1875-76 and 1876-77 listed Robert A. McHenry and Alexander McHenry in the firm of "McHenry & Bro Marble Workers". *The Stockton Daily Independent* newspapers of 1876 had front page advertisements that read, in part, "ROBERT A. McHENRY & BRO MARBLE WORKS, Mantels, Monuments, Tombstones, Plumbers' slabs, on hand and manufactured to order, goods shipped to all parts of the Pacific Coast". A similar full page advertisement was featured on page 5 of the *Statistical County Directory of San Joaquin County, 1878* for "ROBERT A. McHENRY MARBLE WORKS, No. 295 Main Str.". Alexander was no longer mentioned in the 1878 Directory, and neither McHenry was in later directories. Tinkham, in *History of Stanislaus County,* implied that Modesto's Robert McHenry had the middle initial "A".

Page 14. Data are from the Minutes of the Stanislaus County Board of Supervisors, Volume 1.

Page 14. Matilda Hewitt McHenry was born in Steubenville, Ohio, on October 15, 1838.

Page 14-15. Specific references for descriptions of wheat in the San Joaquin Valley are: Bancroft, *History of California Volume XXIV,* pages 24-28, 112-123; Branch, *History of Stanislaus County,* pages 11, 70-71, 73-74; Elias, *Stories of Stanislaus,* pages 18-19; Smith, *Garden of the Sun,* pages 250-253; Tinkham, *History of Stanislaus County,* pages 54-59.

Page 15. The *City and County Directory of San Joaquin, Stanislaus, Merced, and Tuolumne Counties, 1881* listed "Robert McHenry, Cashier Modesto Bank, 2,609 acres". By 1884, the listing in the *Stockton City, San Joaquin, Stanislaus, Calaveras, Tuolumne and Costra Counties Directory* was "McHenry, Robert, Manager the First National Bank of Modesto, res cor I and 15th, 2801 acres".

Page 16. Rogers Hall was built in 1877 by Stimpson Rogers. It was located at 907 H Street, next to the alley, between 9th and 10th. The Hall was upstairs and reportedly accomodated up to 500 persons. It was Modesto's main gathering place until the construction of Plato's Opera House (also an upstairs hall) at 825 10th Street in 1892.

Page 21. The placement of the gas lines in the basement indicates that they were attached to the wooden joists at the time of original construction. Later, some electric wires were placed with the gas lines, which facilitated wiring the house for electricity.

Page 21. A water tank was commonly placed in a separate building, called a tank house. However, Reeder Van Vlear, who was raised near the McHenrys on 14th Street and was a boyhood friend of Merl's, described a different arrangement for the McHenry house. During a 1978 interview, he claimed that there had been two large water storage tanks located in the attic, an early plumbing innovation that was used in some large homes in the East, Midwest, Southern California and the Bay Area. This would have facilitated the installation of a water closet and a cold water basin in the upstairs bathroom. No one has corroborated Van Vlear's story of the attic water tanks, including members of the McHenry family and other former neighbors.

Page 24. In the early 1870s, Charles Henry Huffman was "townsite man" for the Southern Pacific Railroad. According to a description in Outcalt's *History of Merced County*, page 419, Huffman "located nearly all the towns along the railroad through the San Joaquin Valley".

Page 25-26. The Huffman "White House" in Merced was situated on the corner of West North Creek Drive and M Street, which at that time was called Huffman Avenue. After the structure burned down in 1933, the property was sold to Merced attorney C. Ray Robinson who built a large home on the same spot in 1936. That house still stands, occupied by an order of nuns, the Dominican Congregation of St. Catherine of Siena. Two remnants of the Huffman House remain: the original elaborate fence along the street and the Elm trees that line the north bank of the creek.

Page 26. Only five items from the original furnishings are in the McHenry Mansion today: two gilt mirrors of the Eastlake style that were once used over the fireplace mantels, two large landscape oil paintings (one of which was stolen in 1966), and an oak desk with Albert McHenry's initials penciled on the side of a drawer.

Page 28. The quotation by Sol P. Elias is in Tinkham's *History of Stanislaus County*, pages 101-102.

Page 31. Hohenthall and Caswell, in *Streams in a Thirsty Land*, describe Robert McHenry's purchase of the Turlock Irrigation Bonds on pages 64-65.

Page 31. Data are from Volume 1 of the *Modesto Irrigation District Record of Minutes*.

Page 32. City ordinances adopted by the Board of

Trustees from 1884-1889 are in Volume 1, *Record of the Board of Trustees, City of Modesto*.

CHAPTER III
THE WORLD OF MATILDA McHENRY

Page 36. The *Directory of Stockton City and San Joaquin, Stanislaus, Tuolumne & Calaveras Counties, 1893* had a listing for "McHenry, Matilda M. Mrs., res 15th and I" and "McHenry, O., resident the First National Bank and Union Savings Bank, res. Oakdale Road 5 mi out".

Page 37. The second First Presbyterian Church building at 14th and I Streets was dedicated in 1911 and torn down in 1973.

CHAPTER IV
THE WORLD OF ORAMIL McHENRY

Page 41. The Bald Eagle Ranch Victorian home built by Ora McHenry in 1891 still stands in its original location, five miles north of Modesto at 511 Crawford Road.

Pages 43-45. City data are from the minutes in Volumes 2 and 3 of the *Record of the Board of Trustees, City of Modesto*.

Page 45. A page one article in *The Modesto Herald* on August 3, 1911 described the July 29 fire at the Bald Eagle Ranch. "The group of buildings at the Bald Eagle ranch, comprising the slaughter house, abbattoir, ice making and cold storage plant, and the adjoining corrals and pig pens, were totally destroyed by fire on Saturday afternoon. Robert McHenry states that the loss is about $75,000 and the insurance about $25,000". Spontaneous combustion of some crude oil near the buildings apparently started the fire, and the plant, "one of the most complete this side of the Bay", was a total loss. "It is not likely the plant will be rebuilt", the article concluded. Modestan Sidney Smith was a young child when this fire occurred, and he vividly recalls stepping on the hot coals with his bare feet while attempting to follow the lead of older boys who were able to jump over the broad expanse. The Bald Eagle "hotel" for employees also burned down, according to Ora Louise McHenry Condrey.

Page 45. Louise Bilicke McHenry's mother, Caroline (Mrs. Charles) Bilicke, died in Los Angeles in December 1906 from appendicitis. She was about 74.

Page 51. Matilda Conneau (Schafer) was the second child, and first baby girl, born in Modesto following its settlement. The first child was

Benjamin Jones, born in September 1871. Matilda's birth was on September 11, 1872.

Page 51. Annie Conneau Waters' mother, nee Margaret McDonald, was born in Ireland. Her son, George F. Catts (Annie's half brother), became a banker as well as president of Lauxen and Catts Furniture Store and served as Mayor of Stockton in 1901-1903. Margaret died at age 44.

Page 57. The telephone statistics are from an article in the *Stanislaus Weekly News* dated February 5, 1904.

Page 60. Euchre, frequently played at McHenry parties, was once considered the national card game of the United States. It has a long history of mixed ancestry, and similar games were played in Spain, France, and Ireland dating back as far as the 1500s. A deck of 32 cards is used, prepared by discarding all twos to sixes in a regular 52 card deck, and there are usually four players. The object of the game is to win tricks by trumping, so that the opponent is "euchred" or outwitted.

Page 60. *Streams In A Thirsty Land,* (page 234), describes the establishment of the First National Bank of Turlock.

Page 64. Estimates of the size of Ora McHenry's land holdings differ. Tinkham claimed that he owned 20,000 acres in the County (*History of Stanislaus County,* Page 224). Other writers, such as Guinn (*History of the State of California*, page 1531), said he had 12,000 acres. The Bald Eagle Ranch comprised at least 4000 acres and, according to Merl McHenry, covered seven square miles.

Page 64. The Probate File #1034, Stanislaus County Probate Records, having to do with Oramil McHenry estate, includes the following statement: "A former wife, Louise Emma Bilicke McHenry, was paid off in full for any rights to the estate".

CHAPTER VI
THE WORLD OF THE LANGDONS

Page 71-73. City data are taken from minutes recorded in Volume 6, *Record of the Board of Trustees, City of Modesto.*

Page 74. Modesto's First National Bank was sold to the Bank of Italy in 1927, which later became The Bank of America.

Page 75. Several early day Modestans, including Dorothy Rice Magladry, mentioned the predictability of a woman's life during this period. A common routine was: Monday, washing; Tuesday, mending; Wednesday, ironing; Thursday, church activities; Friday, cleaning;

Saturday, cooking for Sunday; Sunday, church and day of rest on the Sabbath.

Page 78. Governor Johnson spoke at the "Auditorium" located at 622 I Street near 7th. The building supposedly held 1800 people, with an additional 500 on the stage.

Page 80. The Plato Medal was awarded to the Modesto High School student who received the highest grades during the senior year. It honored G.D. Plato, who died in June 1915 at age 69. *The History of Modesto High School* (page 14) states that the award was made annually for 21 years beginning in 1917.

CHAPTER VIII
THE ELMWOOD SANITARIUM

Page 86. Reference material about Dr. Kellogg is found in Richard Schaefer's *Legacy, The Heritage of a Unique International Medical Outreach.*

CHAPTER IX
THE APARTMENT HOUSE

Page 91. Several tenants of the Gould Apartments mentioned Gracie (Ethel) Costner, best known as the friendly "bakery girl" at Justesen's Market. Justesen's was owned by Abe Wakefield and Harold Peterson and the Home Market by Len and Erma Hathaway. Mellis Brothers, owned and operated by Dan, James, and Peter Mellis, bought out the G.P. Schafer grocery store, located on I Street between 10th and 11th, in about 1923 according to Spiro Mellis. The 10th Street Piggly-Wiggly, which later became a Safeway, was owned by brothers Harvey and Casper Laws.

Page 92. Matilda Conneau Schafer lived all of her life in Modesto until she moved to the Oakland home of her daughter, Lena Schafer Jaggard, in December 1947. There she died on February 28, 1948.

CHAPTER X
THE RESTORATION

Page 100. The Poets' Corner is under the auspices of the Modesto Culture Commission and was dedicated on May 2, 1982, during ceremonies held on the side veranda of the McHenry Mansion. It is located in the Mansion gardens, marked with a dedication plaque and benches, and is designated as a special place for local poets to write and read their work.

APPENDIX

A. McHenry-Bilicke Wedding

A FASHIONABLE WEDDING,

Features of the McHenry-Bilicke Marriage in Modesto.

[From Thursday's Daily News]

The wedding of Miss Louise Bilicke, only daughter of Mr. and Mrs. G.C. Bilicke, and Ora McHenry, the only son of Mr. and Mrs. Robert McHenry, took place at the Ross House, the home of the bride, yesterday at 11 o'clock, in the presence of a number of relatives and a few intimate friends. The ceremony being performed by Rev. Atherton, of the First Presbyterian Church, of Modesto. Two medium sized rooms in the upper story of the building being connected by an arched doorway and well adapted to the purpose, were chosen as their marriange chambers, and were beautiful decorated. A royal wreath of evergreen hung in graceful scallops around the walls, while trellised vines of the same material surrounded the picture frames, and hung in graceful beauty from several marble topped tables that occupied conspicuous places. Each table supported vases of delicate flowers, whose fragrance were stealing through every nook and corner of the much embellished rooms. The great arched doorway was also much beautified by evergreen trimmings, and from its center hung a huge floral bell made of pale roses and other suitable flowers. The chambers that had been darkened enough to represent twilight, were lighted up by two elegant chandeliers whose brilliant lights were slightly dimmed by a faint skylight, all of which gave a charm of strange beauty to the place. The hour having arrived, the bride and groom took their stand beneath the great floral bell and were supported by Miss Jessie McCormick, first bridesmaid, and J.E. Ward, best man. Miss Lydia Walberg, second bridesmaid, and M.G. Huffman, second groomsman. These were supported on the right by A.C. Bilicke, the bride's brother, and on the left, by Miss Bertie Schleicher, of San Francisco. Rev. Atherton then in a few well chosen remarks, went through with the ceremony and pronounced them man and wife.

The bride wore a beautiful Hilico satin traveling suit, with point lace trimmings. Ornaments, diamonds and pearls.

First bridesmaid wore a dress of black Surah with jet trimmings. Ornaments, turquoise.

Second bridesmaid wore garnet silk with black lace trimmings. Ornaments, turquois, attended by Miss Lydia Walberg in plum velvet. Ornaments, rubies.

The ceremony being over, the party repaired to the dining-room where they were seated and for two hours enjoyed the ample wedding breakfast, eight rounds being served.

The following are the presents received by the bride:

Mrs. and Mrs. McHenry, handsome double case of silver table and tea spoons.

Mr. E. Hastings, handsome case of silver ice cream spoons.

Mrs. Hulbert, a very fine silver cake basket.

A.C. Bilicke, an elegant case containing one dozen beautiful antique silver napkin rings, family relics.

Mrs. Samuel Hewitt, elegant silver napkin ring and castor.

Miss Jesse Nivens, elegant silver-gold lined sugar spoon.

J.R. Hewitt, elegant set of silver knives and forks.

Miss Lula M. Kendall, handsome silver shoe buttoner.

Mr. and Mrs. Seymour, elegant case of silver berry ladles.

J.E. Ward, beautiful case of silver salt cellars gold lining.

Miss Alice H. Marks, elegant silver butter knife.

Mr. and Mrs. W.W. Granger, perfume harp.

H.T. Hewitt, elegant silver butter knife.

Miss Lydia Walberg, a very pretty hand painted tidy.

Miss Bertie Schleisher, a large and beautiful gilt framed oil painting executed by herself.

Miss Bertie Schleisher, a beautiful hand painted satin table scarf.

The happy pair, accompanied by Misses Walberg, Schleisher, McCormick, and others, left for the city on the afternoon train where they will spend the honeymoon season before returning to their already elegant furnished home, some five miles from Modesto. May peace, love, and prosperity attend them through life, are the wishes of the News.

STANISLAUS COUNTY NEWS

FRIDAY.........MARCH 5, 1886.

B. Robert McHenry Funeral

Funeral of Robert McHenry

The funeral of Robert McHenry occurred this afternoon at his late residence in this city. At an early hour, the relations and friends began to arrive, and before the funeral hour, the large parlors were crowded. At two o'clock, the services began, with a beautiful and touching hymn by the choir, followed by prayer from Rev. W. Dennett, of the M.E. Church. Rev. Henry C. Gillingham, of the Presbyterian church, officiated. After dwelling at some length on the nature of death, and the consolations of the religion of Jesus, Mr. Gillingham dismissed his theme and spoke in a very touching manner of the deceased — his long and trying afliction, his patience and resignation. He spoke of the character of Mr. McHenry; his sterling integrity; his candor; his executive ability and his conservative principles of life and morals. He concluded with a short peroration, beautiful in doctrine and touching in thought. Mr. McHenry's remains were interred in the City Cemetery. "Surely, a good man has fallen," seemed to be the sentiment upon the lips of all. The pall-bearers were: Judge A. Hewel, J.S. Alexander, G.D. Plato, Wm. Enslen, Jas. Thompson, H. Voight, J.W. Tulloch, C.A. Stonesifer, C.C. Wright and Gilman Usher. The funeral procession was one of the largest ever seen in Modesto. Some of the floral offerings were very beautiful. As Mr. McHenry had been a helpless invalid for nearly two years, his death has a different influence on the community from what it would had he been stricken down in the full vigor of his life. But, notwithstanding this, his loss will be greatly felt, and his place hard to fill.

Stanislaus County News
June 26, 1890

C. Matilda McHenry Funeral

Funeral of Mrs. McHenry.

The funeral services over the remains of the late Mrs. Matilda M. McHenry took place from the palatial family residence on the corner of Fifteenth and I streets yesterday at 2 p.m., Rev. E.B. Hays officiating. The attendance of relatives and friends of the good lady was unusually large. The floral pieces were many and were very handsome, the magnificent Chancellor casket being almost hidden by them. The plate bore the simple inscription of the name, date of birth, nativity and date of death. The choir consisted of Mr. J.E. Ward, Mrs. W.W. Thompson and Captain R.K. Whitmore and W.F. Targeant, and the bearers of the pall were W.H. Hatton, A.R. Jamison, J.E. Ward, W.B. Wood, James Thompson and L.M. Hickman. The funeral cortege was one of the largest ever held in this city and the remains were solemnly laid to rest beside those of her late husband, Robert McHenry.

Daily Evening News
March 2, 1896

D. St. Patrick's Day Dance

UNIQUE AFFAIR AT McHENRY HOME

The Fancy Dress Party Was an Unusually Brilliant Function

The St. Patrick's day dance on Friday evening at the home of Mrs. and Mrs. O McHenry in this city will stand out as the most unique, gorgeous and delightful affair in the annals of social events in Modesto for many a day as the function was one of unusual splendor and charm.

Several weeks ago invitaitons were issued for a fancy dress party on the evening of the seventeenth and since that time the favored young ladies and gentlemen have been preparing for the event and the result as shown last evening showed that their preparation left nothing to be desired in the matter of fancy dress, as all of them appeared at the best in their many colored robes, and the ensemble made a gorgeous show such as has never before been witnessed in Modesto.

In the neighborhood of forty guests in costume were present, and about thirty others were invited to enjoy the spectacle. Shortly after nine o'clock all were present and the grand march led by J.M. Walthall and Miss Alice Atwood, started an evening of rare pleasure.

The McHenry house must have been designed for just such functions as that within its walls last evening. The rooms are spacious, and admit of the most charming decorations, which last night were exceedingly appropriate, conforming in idea with the day which the affair was designed to celebrate.

The carpets of the large rooms and halls were covered with canvas. In the double doorway hung an immense green bell surrounding an electric light. All of the lights were covered with green crepe paper, making them cast a solft glow over the beautifully decorated rooms. Strands of large paper shamrocks were festooned from the chandeliers to the sides of the room, and flags with the harp of Ireland, bearing the legend, "Erin Go Baugh" completed the decorations of the dancing rooms.

In the hall Cook & Goeffart's orchestra discoursed most pleasing dance music, leaving nothing to be desired in that particular. Green dance programs, also bearing the harp of Erin were distributed and of the fourteen dances and extras thereon, three were devoted to the beautiful figures of the German, the snake, the scarf and the driving figures. The scarfs and ribbons used in the cotillion, also conformed to the color scheme of the evening. Favors were bestowed broadcast, and this new feature at Modesto parties was greatly enjoyed not only by the dancers themselves but by the spectators.

Soon the music had the merry throng gliding over the canvas in the mazes of the dance. Between dances a punch bowl on the enclosed porch furnished delightful refreshment.

Before the entire program had been danced the guests who had been invited to enjoy the sight repaired to the dining room where they partook of most delightful and substantial refreshment.

The last dance of the evening was a ladies' favor, the young ladies presenting their dancing partner with a tiny clay pipe attached to a green ribbon.

About one o'clock the costumers were invited to the dining room and the beautiful decorations there elicited a general expression of pleasure. Streamers of green hung from the chandelier to the corners of the center table, and green place cards told the guests where to sit. Small silken shamrocks were at each place, and the general appearance of the room was of unusual beauty and taste.

The following menu was served and ample justice was done to it by the hungry dancers: Oysters on the half shell, Lobster salad, Turkey, chicken, jelly, olives, salted almonds, Neopolitan ice cream, cakes and confection.

The hour spent at the table passed rapidly with the delicious viands, songs and a few remarks by J.M. Walthall, expressing the sentiments of the entire company in stating that all present were really fortunate in having such royal entertainers as the McHenrys as friends.

It was almost two o'clock before the guests arose from the table and as they took their departure the many and sincere remarks of appreciation combined with the good nights, were received by Mr. and Mrs. McHenry.

Lack of space forbids a description of the many beautiful costumes seen at the affair but an idea may be received from the name, and the statement that the costumes were gorgeous and of great variety all together making a scene of beauty long to be remembered. The selections and the variety of the costumes reflect much credit upon the wearers.

Those present and the characters represented were:

Misses Lettie Conneau, Spanish senorita; Vivian Englehart of Mills Seminary, dawn; Jessie Scoon, popcorn girl; Jessie Jacobsen, Grecian girl; Alice Atwood, maid; Miss Cowery of San Francisco, modern belle; Hattie Logan, Columbia, Lena Conneau, fire queen; Betty Ullman, sailor maid; Sadie Ullman, Japanese girl; Bertha Toombs, college girl with cap and gown; Maude Wildes, colonial girl; Florence Boggs, 16th century girl; Therese Grollman, queen of night; Katherine Hewel, butterfly maid; Edith Kenney, gypsy fortune tellar; Blance Chapel, poppy girl, and Mrs. O. McHenry, Indian maiden. Mesrs. M.F. Reynolds, Mexican vaquero; David Tulloch, Gloomy Gus; W.E. Austin, French hussar; L.B. Carpenter, French cavalier; Claude Shackelford, Chinese mandarin; John Lesher, Don Juan; Irvin Broughton, French Zouare; K.B. Smith, continental soldier; Ernie Conneau, cow puncher; Ed Briggs, Roman charioteer; Robert McHenry, ballet girl; Albert McHenry, Louis XII Cavalier; John Dunn, English swell; H.E. Davis, Gloomy Gus the second; Hannibal Blewett, George Washington; J.M. Walthall, English butler; Hugo Jacobsen, Turkish soldier; Frank Cressey, Charles II courtier; O. McHenry, Indian chief, and Ward Schafer, the Red and Black Mascot.

STANISLAUS WEEKLY NEWS
March 2, 1906

E. Oramil McHenry Funeral

ORA M'HENRY WAS LAID TO REST

Long Cortege Follows Remains of the Banker to the Masonic Cemetery.

Regardless of the inclement weather a large gathering of friends assembled at the McHenry home about 10 o'clock Saturday a.m. to pay their last tribute of respect to O. McHenry. All of the banks and a number of business houses closed from ten until noon, giving all an opportunity of attending Mr. McHenry's funeral.

The religious services were conducted by Rev. H.K. Pitman of the Presbyterian Church, and a vocal quartet composed of Mrs. A.M. Brown, Mrs. G.W. Williamson, W.H. Rhea and J.M. Walthall sang some appropriate selections.

At the particular request of Mr. McHenry, the officiating minister did not enter into an extended eulogy regarding the virtue of the deceased, but he briefly outlined Mr. McHenry's biography, showing what a prominent figure he had been in this county as well as in this portion of the State, and what he had one toward the development of this city and county.

Worthy of special mention are the many beautiful floral tributes sent in by friends of the deceased. A handsome Elk's head was sent in by Mr. McHenry's lodge of that order, and many floral offerings of beautiful designs were received from his frineds in this city and abroad.

After a prayer, the long cortege was formed, and preceded by the Masons proceeded to the Masonic Cemetery, where with the rites of that order impressively read, the remains were interred in the family plot.

A number of friends and relatives from outside of the city attended the funeral and representatives from all of Mr. McHenry's business interests were present.

STANISLAUS WEEKLY NEWS
March 24, 1905

THE FIRST McHENRY MANSION GOVERNING BODIES

THE MODESTO CITY COUNCIL, 1976

Lee H. Davies (Mayor); Clyde H. Dunlap, Robert T. Elliott, Harry T. Kulligian, Peggy Mensinger, Phillip E. Newton, Susan D. Siefkin.

THE MODESTO CULTURE COMMISSION, 1976

Colleen Bare, Jean Dunlap, James Madison, Sal Morales, Natalie Shastid, Ronald Stone, Robert Stuart.

McHENRY MANSION COMMITTEES AND CHAIRPERSONS, 1976

Art in the Mansion, Jean and Raymond Bates; Fireplaces and Mirrors, Sally Crawford and Sue McAllister; Floor Coverings, Ila Reinheimer and Pansy Wilburn; Fund Raising, Willian Hughes; Furnishings, Diane Keller and Jean Pike; Glasses, China and Silver, Susan Filippi and Linda West; Kitchen, Evelyn Joliff and Kathy Menghetti; Landscaping, C. Dwight Wait; Lighting, Marian Bradford and Cindy Brooks; Needlework, Shelia Barton and Natalie Shastid; Public Relations, Maryco Graff; Research, Virginia Bruch; Speakers' Bureau, Linda and Stephen Collins; Use, Richard Lang; Wall Treatment, Lee Nicholson and Florence Wylie; Window Treatment, Margaret Hawkins and Lois Nish.

First McHENRY MANSION FOUNDATION BOARD OF TRUSTEES, 1983 (*Steering Committee)

*Francis Eakin (chairperson), Jean Allewelt, Hugh Barton, James Beard, *Felice Bennett, *Mervyn Bennett, Richard Brew, Nancy Carrade, Charles Crivelli, Lee Davies, *Shirley Elke, *Louis Friedman, *John Hodge, Clyda Hudelson, Diane Keller, David Kilby, *Lois Mayol, Larry McCormick, Wanda Melson, Kathy Menghetti, Michael Mensinger, Norman Moseley, Jean Pike, Lawrence R. Robinson, Jr., *Armour Smith, Ronald Stone, Michael Sturtevant, Keith Vogt, Anne Woolley.

BIBLIOGRAPHY AND RESOURCES

BOOKS

Annear, Margaret L.; Florcken, Herbert G.; and Baker, Hugh. *A Brief History of Stanislaus County*, Stanislaus County Schools, Modesto, California 1950

Benziger, Jeffery. *Oakdale Historical Journal*, Jeffery B. Benziger, 1982.

Bancroft, Hubert H. *The Works of Hubert Howe Bancroft, Vol. XXIV, History of California, Vol. VII, 1860-1890*, The History Company, San Francisco, 1890.

Brotherton, I.N. "Jack". *Annals of Stanislaus County, Volume I*, River Towns and Ferries, Western Tanager Press, Santa Cruz, 1982.

Dix, Mrs. Ray. *Cemetery Records of Stanislaus County*, Downey Historical Society, Modesto, 1960.

Elias, Sol P. *Stories of Stanislaus*, privately printed, Modesto, California, 1924.

Florcken, Herbert G. *A Brief History of Stanislaus County, Volume 2*, unpublished manuscript, 1954.

Guinn, J.M. *History of the State of California and Biographical Record of the San Joaquin Valley*, The chapman Publishing Company, Chicago, 1905.

Herbert, Ruth Hewitt and Groves, Aileen. *The History of Old Farmington*, privately printed, Farmington, California, undated.

Herndon, Carroll Ray. *Stanislaus County 1854-1954 A Century of Growth*, Stanislaus County Schools, 1955.

The History of Modesto High School, 1883-1983, privately printed, 1983.

Hohenthall, Helen and Caswell, John (ed). *Streams In A Thirsty Land*, A History of the Turlock Region, City of Turlock, 1972.

Illustrated Atlas and History of Yolo County, California. De Pue and Company, San Francisco, 1879.

Illustrated History of San Joaquin County, California. The Lewis Publishing Company, Chicago, 1890.

Index to the 1850 Census of The State of California. Compiled by Alan P. Bowman, Genealogical Publishing Company, Inc., Baltimore, 1972.

Jackson, Ronald & Teeples, Gary. *California 1850 Census Index*, Accelerated Indexing Systems Inc., Utah, 1978.

Kirker, Harold. *California's Architectural Frontier*, Russell & Russell Publishers, New York, 1970.

Maino, Jeannette Gould (ed). *One Hundred Years*, Belt Printing Company, Modesto, California, 1970.

Memorial and Biographical History of Northern California, The Lewis Publishing Company, Chicago, 1891.

Outcalt, John. *History of Merced County,* Historic Record Co., Los Angeles, California, 1925.

Parker, J. Carlyle (ed). *Memorial and Biographical History, Merced, Stanislaus, Calaveras, Tuolumne and Mariposa Counties California,* McHenry Museum of Art and History, Modesto, California, 1980.

Parker, Nathan C. *Personal Name Index to the 1856 City Directories of California,* Gale Research Col., Michigan, 1980.

Schafer, Richard A. *Legacy, The Heritage of a Unique International Medical Outreach,* Pacific Press Publishing Association, Mountain View, California, 1978.

Smith, Wallace. *Garden of The Sun,* fourth edition, A-1 Printers, Fresno, California, 1960.

Silverberg, Robert. *John Muir,* G.P. Putnam's Sons, New York, 1972.

Stanford Alumni Association. *Stanford Alumni 1891-1955,* Volume I, Stanford University Press, Stanford, California, 1956.

Thompson, Thomas H. and West, Albert A. *History of San Joaquin County 1879,* Howell-North Books, Berkeley, CA 1968.

Tennent, Esther M. *California Was Built,* Vantage Press, New York, 1965.

Tinkham, George H. *History of San Joaquin County, California, With Biographical Sketches,* Historic Record Company, Los Angeles, California 1923.

_____ *History of Stanislaus County,* Historic Record Company, Los Angeles, California, 1921.

_____ *A History of Stockton,* W.M. Hinton & Company, 1880.

Vasche, Joseph Burton. *The Story of Our County,* Stanislaus County Schools, 1942.

Wood, R. Coke and Covello, Leonard. *Stockton Memories,* Valley Publishers, Fresno, 1977.

CITY AND COUNTY DIRECTORIES

Bishops Stockton Directory for 1876-1877, Business Directory, compiled by D.M. Bishop & Company, published by B.C. Vandall, September 1876.

California State Business Directory 1875-1876, D.M. Bishop & Company, San Francisco, 1876.

California State Gazetteer and Business Directory, 1890, R.L. Polk & Company, 1890.

City and County Directory of San Joaquin, Stanislaus, Merced, and Tuolumne Counties, L.M. McKinney & Co., San Francisco, April 1881.

Directory of Stockton City and San Joaquin, Stanislaus, Tuolumne, & Calaveras Counties, F.M. Husted, Publishing, San Francisco, 1893.
Modesto City and Stanislaus County Directory, 15 vols., 1910-1924, Polk-Husted Directory Company, Sacramento, California.

Polk's Directory of Modesto, Turlock, & Stanislaus County, 5 vols., 1925-1929, R.L. Polk & Company, San Francisco, California.

Polk's Modesto and Turlock City Directory Including Stanislaus County, 21 vols., 1930-1950, R.L. Polk & Company, San Francisco.

Polk's Modesto City Directory, 22 vols., 1951-1972, R.L. Polk & Company, Monterey Park, Los Angeles, Calfiornia.

San Joaquin County Directory for 1871-1872, County Directory Publishing Company, Sacramento, 1871.

Statistical County Directory of San Joaquin County, D.H. Berdine, Stockton, California, 1878.

Stockton City, San Joaquin, Stanislaus, Calaveras, Tuolumne, and Costra Counties Directory, L.M. McKinney & Co., San Francisco, 1884.

Stockton City Directory 1856, Harris, Joseph & Company, San Francisco, 1856.

Stockton City Directory, 1873-74, W.D. Root & Co., 1873.

Stockton City and County Directory, 1883-1884, J.W. Smith & Co., San Francisco, 1884.

ARTICLES, JOURNALS, AND THESIS

Betrami, Albert Peter. "Modesto Irrigation District: A Study In Local Resources and Administration". Unpublished Masters Thesis, 1955.

Bruch, Virginia. "Popular Story Says Mansion Was Built 'Bigger For Less' To Win A Friendly Bet", *The Stanislaus Stepping Stones, Quarterly Bulletin of the Stanislaus County Historical Society,* Volume 3, Number 1, Spring, 1979.

California Architect and Building News, San Francisco Architectural Publishing Company, 1880-1890.

Graham, Robert M. "An Epic Of Water And Power. A History Of The Modesto Irrigation District". Unpublished Masters Thesis, College of the Pacific, Stockton, 1946.

Keller, Diane and Pike, Jean. "McHenry Mansion Furniture", unpublished article, 1979.

Ortiz, Maria. "James Porteous, Fresno's Forgotten Inventor", *Fresno-Past & Present, The Journal of the Fresno City and County Historical Society,* Winter 1981. (Volume 23, Number 4)

Lang, Judith. "The Glory of Early Modesto", *Valley Views,* March, 1980.

Nish, Lois. McHenry family research materials at the McHenry Museum of Arts and History, Modesto.

Modesto Bee. *Centennial Edition,* July 3, 1970.

Stanislaus Board of Trade. *Modesto-Turlock Irrigation District c. 1910.*

NEWSPAPERS

Merced Star
Merced Sun Star
Modesto Bee
Modesto Daily Evening News
Modesto Morning Herald
Sacramento Record Union
San Francisco Call
San Francisco Chronicle
San Joaquin Daily Republican

Stanislaus Evening News
Stanislaus Weekly News
Stockton Daily Evening Herald
Stockton Daily Evening Record
Stockton Daily Mail
Stockton Independent
Stockton Republican
Tuolumne City Weekly

INTERVIEWS

(All interviews were done by the author except for those of Lena Schafer Jaggard and Reeder Van Vlear. Goldie Davis, Merl McHenry and Mary Aline Polk were also interviewed by others [taped and/or transcribed] as well as by the author, as indicated. Several persons were interviewed by mail, including some McHenry family members, Norma Norberto, and Mary Aline Polk. Some of those interviewed contributed important background material pertaining to Modesto history and the times, rather than family data).

Baker, Jesse Stinson
Behr, Margaret Maze
Bradford, Clarkson B., Jr.
Condrey, Ora Louise McHenry
Conneau, Arthur Ernest, Jr.
Cooper, Dr. John
Crabtree, Derald and Dorothy
Davis, Lee H.
Florcken, Herbert G.
Flygare, Rosamond Raynor
Davis, Goldie, by Colleen Bare, Roselle
   Gant, Ruth Kimber, and Judith Lang
Eichel, Marina
Gant, Roselle Davis
Giovanetti, Mae
Hartwich, Isabel Warren
Herbert, Ruth Hewitt
Jaggard, Lena Schafer Maze, by Diane
   Keller and Jean Pike
Jones, Lois Huffman
McHenry, Jack Robert

McHenry, Merl by Colleen Bare and
   Wayne Mathis
McHenry, Raefield Albert
McHenry, Robert Wesley
Magladry, Dorothy Rice
Medlin, Clara Bridges
Melgard, Sally Scharnberg
Murchie, Elmer
Norberto, Norma F.
Pagen, Bobbe Jean McHenry Pauley
Polk, Mary Aline, by Colleen Bare and
   Jeannette Maino
Price, Marguerite Johnson
Raleigh, Gita Linhares
Smith, Esther Osterberg
Smith, Paul H.
Smith, Sidney
Stanley, Harriett Kirkman
Thompson, Elaine Crow
Van Vlear, Reeder by Wayne Mathes

ADDITIONAL RESOURCES INCLUDING LIBRARIES

Bancroft Library, Berkley
California State Historical Library,
   Sacramento
California State Historical Society,
   Schubert Library, San Francisco
Fresno County Free Library
Haggin Museum, Petzinger Library,
   Stockton
Holt-Atherton Pacific Center for Western
   Studies, U. of the Pacific, Stockton
Masonic (Acacia) Cemetery Records
Masonic Lodge #206 Records
Merced County Library
Merced County Museum
McHenry Museum of Arts and History
Modesto City minutes in *Record of*

Modesto Board of Trustees, Volumes 1-6,
   1884-1911
Modesto City minutes in *Record of
   Modesto City Council*, Volumes 6-8,
   1911-1920
Modesto Irrigation District *Minutes of the
   Board of Directors*
San Francisco Public Library
Stanislaus County Board of Supervisors,
   Minutes, Volumes 1, 2, 3
Stanislaus County Library
Stanislaus County Probate Records
Stanislaus County Schools
Stockton-San Joaquin County Public
   Library
Ticor Title Company

INDEX

THE AUTHOR

Colleen Stanley Bare is a free-lance writer and photographer with a special interest in the McHenry Mansion and Modesto history. As chairman of the Modesto Culture Commission from 1976 to 1984, she was active in the McHenry Mansion restoration planning from its very beginning.

Her writing career includes the publication of a number of children's books, illustrated with her photography (publisher Dodd, Mead & Company, Inc.), including *Sea Lions, Guinea Pigs Don't Read Books, Tree Squirrels,* and *Rabbits and Hares.* She has had nearly 200 articles published in popular magazines and newspapers, and hundreds of her poems have appeared in such publications as *Good Housekeeping, McCalls, Ladies Home Journal, Saturday Evening Post, Christian Science Monitor,* etc.

The author has lived most of her life in Modesto and was educated in local schools as well as at Stanford University (A.B., Psychology) and the University of California, Berkeley (M.A., Educational Psychology). She has actively participated in Modesto community affairs, with many years of service on school and city government committees and ten years on the Modesto Culture Commission.

The famous Cupola.

The McHenry Mansion, Modesto's Heritage.

PRINTING CREDITS

Printed in Modesto, California
by Compass Maps and Publications (Compass Maps, Inc.)
Cover Design: Karen Scofield
Cover Photo: Colleen Stanley Bare
Book Design: Shirley Elke
Typeface: Tiffany Medium and Heavy
Typographer: Sheila Jean Robinson
Color Separations: Quadra Color, Sacramemto, California
Cover Stock: Lusterkote coated one side Basis .010
Text Stock: Warren Lustro Dull 80 lb.
Bindery: Cardoza-James Bindery Company,
San Francisco, California